DATE DUE			
MAY 1 5 1993	JAN 1 5 '99		
SEP 1 5 1993			
APR 1 5 1996			
MAY 2 3 1996			
JUN 1 8 1996			
MAY 1 '97			
JUL 9 '07			
DEC.1 1997			
AUG 1 7 98			

RANCHING TRADITIONS

RANCHING TRADITIONS

LEGACY OF THE AMERICAN WEST

**PHOTOGRAPHS BY
KATHLEEN JO RYAN**

**ESSAYS BY
REUBEN ALBAUGH,
BAXTER BLACK, HAL CANNON,
DAVID DARY, GRETEL EHRLICH,
JOHN R. ERICKSON,
TERESA JORDAN, ELMER KELTON,
WILLIAM KITTREDGE, GUY LOGSDON,
KATHLEEN JO RYAN, DICK SPENCER,
AND RANDY WITTE**

**ABBEVILLE PRESS
PUBLISHERS
NEW YORK**

HALF-TITLE PAGE: Rawhide riata, Big Loop rodeo, Jordon Valley, Oregon; FRONTIS-PIECE: Cowboy and horses, Sombrero Ranch horse drive, Colorado; SPREAD, PAGES 4–5: Winter moonrise over Fish Creek Ranch, Russell Ranches' Nevada headquarters; FACING COPYRIGHT PAGE: Rocky Mountain autumn in Colorado; FACING SPONSOR'S PAGE: Beaver Meadows Ranch, Montana; TABLE OF CONTENTS: Father and son working cattle in northeastern Nevada.

INSET ILLUSTRATIONS

PAGE 13: Antlers mounted on the wall at the C S Ranch, Cimarron, New Mexico; PAGE 28: Rusted wagon rigging, Noffsinger Ranches, Walden, Colorado; PAGE 45: Chaps, or "leggin's"; PAGE 61: Typical Texas spur; PAGE 79: Leather wrapped around the horn to keep the rope from slipping when dally roping; PAGE 99: Red Angus calf; PAGE 113: "White-face" calf; PAGE 131: Baling twine has almost completely replaced wire for baling hay; PAGE 149: Black bally cow, the classic cross of the Black Angus and Hereford breeds; PAGE 171: Stamped leather, King Saddlery, Sheridan, Wyoming; PAGE 191: "Sampler" musical pageant; PAGE 211: Rawhide bosals displayed at the Big Loop Rodeo, Jordon Valley, Oregon (A bosal is a nosepiece, often made of braided rawhide or latigo, that is part of a hackamore.); PAGE 235: Bareback riding at the Cheyenne Frontier Days, Wyoming.

PAGES 280–81: Beaver Meadows Ranch, Montana

First, this book is dedicated to the memory of my loving parents, John William and Edith Alta Ryan, for their selfless commitment to giving me their best and always seeing the best in me; it was their tender loving guidance, unconditional love, support, and encouragement to do whatever I could dream of doing that instilled in me the confidence to fulfill my dreams.

This is also dedicated to my sister, Mischel Denise Ryan, for her extraordinary friendship, unconditional love, and business management; without her generous commitment I could not have completed this book. To my brother, John Michael Ryan, who is always ready with words of wisdom and gentle counsel; and for his love, humor, and inspiration. And to the Smith family, Horace, Renie, Kim, Agee, and Vicky, for inspiring me to produce this book.

Editor: Alan Axelrod
Designer: Julie Rauer
Production editor: Robin James
Production manager: Dana Cole

First edition

Published in the United States of America by Abbeville Press, Inc.

"Between the Lines," reprinted on pp. 178–79, © Bruce Kiskaddon
Excerpt from "Cattle Drive, 1988," reprinted on pp. 188–89, © C. J. Hadley
Photo of Charlie Daniels, p. 261, by Mike Rutherford

Library of Congress Cataloging-in-Publication Data

Ryan, Kathleen, 1946–
Ranching traditions : legacy of the American West / photographs by Kathleen Jo Ryan : essays by Reuben Albaugh...[et al.].
p. cm.
Includes index.
ISBN 0-90659-911-6 : $49.95
1. Ranch life—West (U.S.) 2. Cowboys—West (U.S.) 3. West (U.S.)—Social life and customs. 4. Ranch life—West (U.S.)—Pictorial works. 5. Cowboys—West (U.S.)—Pictorial works. 6. West (U.S.)—Social life and customs—Pictorial works. I. Title.
F596.R95 1990   88-7042
978—dc20   CIP

The generous support of these sponsors and contributors made this book possible. This page is an opportunity to thank each individual and company publicly for their vision and belief in the potential of this book. The decision of each individual and company to participate was based on a personal and corporate dedication to the ranching way of life. Thank you to all.

PRIMARY CORPORATE SPONSORS

EASTMAN KODAK COMPANY
MSD AGVET, Division of Merck & Co., Inc.

SPONSORS

MRS. JACK A. HARRIS
JOHN B. STETSON COMPANY
JOHN ASCUAGA'S NUGGET HOTEL–CASINO
THE NOCONA BOOT COMPANY
RUSSELL RANCHES
LEVI STRAUSS & CO.
THE GATES CORPORATION
SHEPLERS WESTERN WEAR
BEEF: The Business Paper of the Cattle Industry
CABIN FEVER ENTERTAINMENT, INC.

HONOR ROLL CONTRIBUTORS

COTTONWOOD RANCH
J. R. SIMPLOT COMPANY
J. M. CAPRIOLA CO.
SCHAEFER, OUTFITTER
NATIONAL WESTERN STOCK SHOW & RODEO
KING'S SADDLERY / KING ROPES
COLORADO BEEF COUNCIL
NICK PETRY–THE PETRY COMPANY
MR. & MRS. CEBORN A. HANSON
JACK SPARROWK–SPARROWK LIVESTOCK
CALIFORNIA BEEF COUNCIL
MR. & MRS. JACK COOKE
CLARK COMPANY
C S RANCH
R. A. BROWN RANCH
CONTINENTAL GRAIN COMPANY

CONTENTS

PREFACE

KATHLEEN JO RYAN

The seed for this book was planted when I was about twelve and our family moved to four acres in rural Sacramento County, California. For eight years I raised and groomed my 4-H cattle and sheep. I shared hay, stalls, and show rings at local and county fairs with my 4-H friends, the sons and daughters of ranchers in Northern California. I thrived, learning leadership skills, the value of personal accountability, and the joy of working with livestock out under open skies.

In light of our family background this was a novel upbringing. Even though my father was a career Air Force officer, my parents made the decision that their children would be raised in the country, not on a military base. So they bought four acres, and we started from scratch, building barns, putting up fences, and purchasing livestock. While Dad was the architect and grew an incredible garden, Mom was the manager of our daily operation. We raised whatever livestock and animals we wanted. The ranch certainly did not produce income, but nobody ever mentioned that—or, in fact, the hardship it *put* on the family income.

Those years in the country formed the basis and foundation of my personal values. When I entered college, I sold my Black Angus cow to buy my first car. Following college, I traveled considerably for a number of years, working in five states. By 1973, I had settled into an executive job in San Francisco, and I became quite absorbed in my executive status. Actually, looking back, it was not

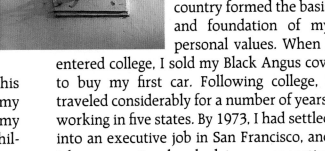

Lacey
Ranch cowboy

Foothills,
central California

Jarbidge
Wilderness Area, northeastern
Nevada
opposite

the position but, rather, self-absorption that shaped my perspective. Photography became my personal outlet and form of creative expression.

In 1974, through friends, I was offered the chance to photograph a traditional ranch rodeo in Northeastern, Nevada. The rodeo was an annual Fourth of July celebration on the Smith family's Cottonwood Ranch, and it would bring together all the ranch families in the O'Neill Basin. The opportunity was too appealing to turn down, and I

accepted it as my first photographic assignment.

The Smith family was wonderful, warm, and accepting. The ranch, with no phone, was seventy miles from the nearest town, Wells, Nevada. The rodeo brought together about two hundred neighbors, some traveling as far as ninety miles. Everyone was friendly and gracious. It was a step back in time and into my own past. Under the moonlight, the cowboys drank beer, told stories, and took turns keeping the embers hot in a big open pit, while lamb, pork, and a side of beef cooked overnight. Life was simple, with a profound sense of integrity— a contrast to my city life. On a back-road tour of the ranch I saw and photographed the most unspoiled open country that I had ever seen. It was my reintroduction to the West.

When I returned to San Francisco, the city looked and felt different. And while it didn't take me long to return to my old patterns and attitudes, a little voice had started in my head, reminding me there was more to life than what I was living day to day. In 1976, the little voice became louder. My heart missed the substance I had experienced at Cottonwood Ranch, so I returned to visit the Smith family once again.

That summer began an annual pilgrimage to the ranch, and each year I brought with me a whole package of city stresses, schedules, and a cluttered state of mind. Getting there required driving twelve hours across Nevada, including an hour on the Smiths' gravel road. On a ridge just above the ranch I would stop, get out of my car, and just listen. Standing on this ridge, straining to hear noises, it was hard to believe there was any place in the world without the sounds of civilization. To this day, on every trip to and from the ranch, I still stop just to experience that total quiet.

The Smiths became my adopted family, and within hours of my arrival we would catch up on our lives. At night, before bed, I stood outside to soak in the brilliance of stars that lit up the sky from horizon to horizon. Early the next morning I would be mounted on a patient "dude" horse and join whatever ranch work needed to be done. In time, I improved ever so slightly, eventually earning the right to ride better

Quarter
Horse foal, R. A. Brown Ranch,
Throckmorton, Texas

New Mexico
windmill at sunset

horses. It was a thrill to ride a working cow horse that had instincts superior to mine. As my ability and confidence grew, I was given larger areas of the open range to cover when we worked cattle or horses. It was delightful to see my little improvements from one year to the next, and each experience brought me into contact with an aspect of life that I was missing in the city.

The ranch and open range gave me a sense of reality that contrasted with city life. I developed a new awareness of traditional values. Coming from the world of man-made schedules, it was enlightening to recognize the integrity of nature's timetable.

Through the years, the Smiths and I have discussed the changing cattle business and the precarious position of family ranching. The cattle market had bottomed out in 1973, and the following years were lean, too, requiring hard decisions. We discussed how they could diversify with recreational pack trips into the adjacent Jarbidge National Wilderness, where the family had taken hunters for years. These discussions were always difficult because of their passion and commitment to continue ranching in the tradition of three generations. It had been the family's dream to have the five children and *their* families continue as a part of the ranch operation, each with their own home on the ranch. It was painful to see the dream unraveling. The harsh realities and economics of the cattle industry had been cruel. But the Smiths continued to pursue the dream and are making it work by supplementing the ranching operation with a successful pack-trip business.

In 1982 I began a book on Ireland. The next three years were spent traveling from my home in California to New York and Ireland, completely immersing myself in Irish culture. My communication with the Smith ranch was reduced to Christmas letters and postcards, and *Irish Traditions* was published in 1985.

Contemplating my next project, it struck me that, in the last couple of decades, much of our western heritage had been ignored by a society seeking the accumulation of position and possessions. Traditional family structure and security were breaking down, and personal values seemed to be disintegrating with frightening speed. I realized that the traditional ranching life-style represented an opportunity to rediscover these values, and I wanted to document the life and the traditions of families like the Smiths. *Ranching Traditions: Legacy of the Ameri-*

can *West* became a way for me to celebrate this precious family and my own western background.

I began the project in January 1986. The American public, in its long and passionate affair with the wide-open spaces and rugged life of the West, had made heroes of the cowboys, but had largely ignored the rancher. The fact that seemed to have been lost was that cowboys always worked *for* ranchers. My desire was to create a book that offered insight into one of our country's oldest traditions through a visual and literary journal of ranch life in the West.

Within a month of my first photographing trip, I learned that my mother had a brain tumor and was scheduled for surgery. I dropped everything and joined her and my father—who was himself declining in health—at their home in Washington. It was heart-wrenching to watch these two devoted, loving people saying goodbye after forty-three years of marriage. Mother died a month after her surgery.

I picked up my emotional pieces and set out again on my ranching project. In January 1987, Dad was greatly improved and I was filled with renewed commitment and the freshness of the New Year. The ranch families I was meeting were a tremendous support, and the project was as wonderful as I had imagined it would be. I returned to my home in California in February with a solid momentum finally established. The morning after my return, I learned that my father had died peacefully in his sleep. There are no words to describe the emotions of this time.

Although death is an inevitable part of life, it is one experience we are never prepared for. In fact, in our culture, death is often denied, so that, when it does touch

your life, there is no real, established support. Being the eldest and losing both parents is an abrupt passage. Extraordinary vulnerabilities and fears suddenly threaten, as if in a childhood nightmare. Moreover, Dad's death marked, eleven months to the day, the death of one of my dearest and closest friends. In less than a year, I had lost three cornerstones of my life.

I was slow to acknowledge the impact of my grief. I appeared to be functioning effectively and continuing on my path. However, there was pain just beneath the surface. Grief is a powerful process that does not indulge the ego in its self-sufficiency for very long. At some point you have to love away the pain within yourself, acknowledge its depth, and respect your efforts to deal with new and overwhelming emotions. As difficult and frightening as it was, there were insights and enlightenment to be gained.

I decided to move to the family home

Hereford cows with winter feed (which the rancher grows in the summer), Gunnison, Colorado

in Washington and packed up a life of fifteen years. I had yet to learn about respecting my own grief and appreciating myself for my efforts. I fought hard to maintain the "superwoman" image of myself—being strong and willful without tenderness. My body did not respond positively to being forced into action. I was not ready to travel, but I did so anyway.

Within a week, I collapsed in a strange town, miles from anyone I knew. It was quite an irony: I was in a beautiful place, too weak and too sick to care. Finally, I recognized the depth of my emotional crisis and loss in my life and drove to the Smiths' ranch to heal. For the first time I actually looked in the mirror and saw the gray, tired face—eyes filled with sadness and pain—an exhausted, fragile woman overwhelmed with grief. I spent the next weeks sleeping, eating ranch beef, letting myself be loved by the Smiths, while learning to be tender with myself. My intolerance for my own

Old barn at the foot of the Grand Tetons, Jackson Hole, Wyoming

needs softened, and I began to heal inside with a gentleness of spirit. My strength returned. Within a couple of weeks, I was back in the saddle working ten-hour days on horseback. I regained momentum, and with renewed spirit and enthusiasm, was back on the road.

Sometimes the open range country of the West is not particularly inviting. There are road signs posted that warn, "No services for the next 120 miles." Except for an occasional dwelling dotted along the horizon, it appears that there is nothing, and that can be forbidding—until you venture out and feel the freedom and the caress of open space. It is difficult to describe because so few people have a frame of reference to encompass this spaciousness. Due to the apparent emptiness of this vast open country, it is easy to assume that you can see it all. Only when you look beyond the obvious, without expectation, you can begin to discover and appreciate this western landscape.

When you work cattle on the open range, you are assigned your own piece of the West. There is never any discussion about your ability to handle the job; you just do it. The most frequent work is "gathering," which is to round up all the cattle in an obscurely defined area, usually farther than you can see from any given point. You will not see another human again until your work is almost done, and for hours the only signs of humanity will be a fence line and an occasional gate. You just hope that you will find your way.

Spending hours on the open range is not romantic or mystical, but rather a solitary, contemplative experience that either fosters confidence or fear. To the infrequent visitor it all looks very much alike; however,

Thunderstorm
in northern New Mexico

Chuck and Kay
Sylvester's Circle Bar Ranch, open-
range country, Alcova, Wyoming

A Nevada winterscape: open range and snow on the sage

Moorhouse Ranch cowboy washing the pots and pans after a day of working cattle, Hall County, Texas

to a rancher or cowboy who has lived and worked the open range, every inch is as identifiable and well known as their own home. Left alone to gather rather elusive cattle, you have plenty of time to ponder the total isolation and possible perils—rattlesnakes, badger holes, a spooked horse. Just you, a good cow horse, and—if you are lucky—a working stock-dog companion, alone for as far as the eye can see.

Being alone in the vastness of open range, which exists in only a few places on earth, is at once solitary and universal. It is a profound experience in its simplicity. At first it seems very empty and still, then suddenly you realize that everything is in movement, in the process of growing or dying: a cactus blooming or the decaying carcass from a coyote kill. It is a full orchestra, playing a symphony of the infinite, while you, as the uninvited guest, gingerly step through. The most profound

thought that I have had while out on the range for hours on horseback is that I am very small.

Ranchers are a different breed. That is what makes this project so distinctive. Although threatened by economics and change, ranchers still live and work in the tradition of their ancestors. Ranching is an exclusive life of shared experiences, a study of contrasts: the heroic action of life-and-death moments, the repetition of daily chores, the elegance of simple beauty, the profound drama of natural phenomena, the extreme isolation, the fierce independence and individuality, the trust of families and friends depending upon one another for daily conversation, companionship, and survival. Ranchers are family people; in fact, family life is vital to their survival. If they are alone, it is usually the result of death of a partner or family member.

Ask a rancher to tell you about his life, land, and livestock, and he will tell you a love story, a story of appreciation and gratitude, of productivity and potential. If you ask for more, he will just take you out and let you experience it for yourself with-

out explanation or editorial comments.

Some of the most delightful time during this journey has been spent in the front seat of a pickup or Suburban, bouncing around on a ranch tour. It is a time of absolute joy for each rancher to showcase his or her land and livestock. It is more than pride, and it is not ownership. It is far more delicate and intimate—a tender love, brimming with admiration, respect and appreciation, a gracious recognition of what is bigger and beyond.

For me, calving is a magical season. The hours are grueling, as ranchers and cowboys check cows about every two to six hours, twenty-four hours a day, for about sixty days straight. One of my treasured experiences was during spring calving at a ranch in the Colorado Rockies. We were up each day at four A.M. for the first check; it took about two hours to check a thousand cows and heifers. The rancher would negotiate the frozen ground and snow drifts with his small pick-up, seeking out a cow that might have isolated herself in preparation for giving birth. He would shine a hand-held spotlight on each cow he thought might be getting ready; he would check her eyes, see how she was breathing, and mentally register her general condition so he could guage her progress in a few hours. The time between the calf checks depended upon the number of cows calving, if any calves had to be pulled, the weather, and any number of other unforeseen situations. Along with this calving schedule, all other winter ranch activity continues, including feeding twice a day from a feed wagon, fixing equipment, gates, fences, and so on.

To be present at the birth of another living, breathing creature is to witness the miracle and power of life giving life. Ranchers live with this reality daily, and they carry on in their unflappable style. Rarely does any event break their stride.

Every ranch crisis requires immediate action. A rancher's personal commitment keeps him going in spite of exhaustion or even injury. It is this genuine accountability to someone or something outside of oneself that makes ranchers and cowboys different from other people. This attitude has nothing to do with who owns the livestock, equipment, or ranch. Ranchers put the care and comfort of their livestock before their own. It is not considered a sacrifice; it is simply the "right" thing to do. No one tells them that; they just know it. It is a sense of priority, an understanding of the proper action for the moment, with a willingness to accept the consequences.

Cattle drives are legendary in the West, but the semi-trailer truck has made them almost a thing of the past. Only a few ranchers still drive their cattle on horseback from winter range to summer range and back, and it is indeed enchanting to rise before dawn, saddle up in the dark, and wait for the first hint of light. You ride out, trusting your horse to see where you are going, since you cannot. There is something very equal about people when they get up before the sun. All pretense and illusion evaporate. A bond is established, a shared commitment, and everyone starts the day joined in a lightly spiritual way, even total strangers. It stays with you throughout the

day and into the evening, when everyone drags in tired and dusty, yet refreshed. There is also that exhilarating time, when the temperature drops slightly just before dawn. It invigorates the soul. Your cattle work is always slower than you expect, and the day is begun at a pace dictated by the very animal that you are supposed to be controlling. I was very fortunate to participate in several of these drives, and each was an extraordinary adventure.

The last cattle drive I worked was delightful. In four days we moved eleven hundred mother cows sixty miles with a cowboy crew of ten. Each day had its own magic, with fresh high-desert air, the fragrance of sage crushed under hooves, an occasional voice drifting across the wind, and the meditative sound of saddle leather creaking while the feet of cattle and horses shuffled through the rocks and dirt. Six to eight hours in the saddle each day: it was at once refreshing and exhausting. We started out with a soft warm breeze, and by day four had graduated to thirty-five-mile-an-hour winds and blowing dust.

Driving cattle is a test of endurance. We had endless hours of breathing dust, wondering if these "girls" would ever make it. Then a cranky cow with independent thinking would bring out the "cowboy" in all of us. For me, the best contrast was to have been in the midst of Los Angeles traffic one day, and on horseback on the open range the next.

Another highlight was the happy discovery that chivalry is still alive and well in the West. I was out with a cowboy crew in West Texas while they were working cattle, bringing in cows that had been on the range for the winter. Because of the great horses I was given to ride, I was entirely confident that I could contribute to

Tom Hudson,
Russell Ranch cowboy, and friend
offer an equine howdy, Diamond
Valley, Nevada

the effort. On one particular occasion, a cranky old cow refused to go through the gate into the corral. At the last second she reversed her direction and headed out past the cowboy herding her, coming straight toward me. Alas, I felt I could save the moment and demonstrate that I was not just a photographer. I let out a whoop and wildly waved my arms, sure that this cow would respect my heroic effort and turn back. Instead, she hit turbo-boost and shot past me, giving the cowboy in hot pursuit a long, rambunctious ride. Needless to say, I felt very silly and humbled. When the cowboy returned and successfully penned the cow, I weakly apologized. With all the grace and charm of a country gentleman, he tipped his hat and said, "Well, Ma'am, if she had only stopped long enough to hear what you had to say, I could have caught up."

In developing the concept for this book, I wanted to present through the text and photography the perspective of ranching as a way of life. Each of the writers was selected for his or her expertise, as well as personal experience and background in ranching. As the book evolved and the essays were completed, something was still missing. I was meeting all of these extraordinary ranchers, yet I had made no provision for their direct participation in the book.

Most ranchers do not choose writing as a form of communication, and often they prefer not to explain or describe their lives at all. Here was a challenge: to give them a direct voice in the book. I added a chapter originally titled "American Heroes," a collection of responses to the question, "Why do you choose a ranch way of life?" The answers are as independent and individual as the people themselves, reflecting a continuity of wisdom, humility, humor, and simple truths. But many of my contributors expressed resistance to the title, because they do not see themselves as heroes. For this reason the final chapter is now titled, "The Reluctant Heroes." These ranchers are truly heroes, but their modesty resists such acknowledgment. The flexibility required to cope with the unpredictable, unforgiving, and sometimes brutal environment, combined with unflinching personal accountability, reflects their strength, courage, and heroic character.

A blessing of this journey has been the joy and companionship of my travel partner. He is intelligent, intuitive, and unconditional in his love. His natural instincts for working livestock are awe inspiring. I am humbled by the reality that all I have taught him is rudimentary manners. One rancher asked me how it felt to be traveling with a dog smarter than I was. Star is from a family of award-winning Border collies, and he knows it. He has charmed his way through twelve western states, creating a growing fan club along the way. He has worked the cattle drives, ridden snowmobiles and four wheelers, and traveled 80,000 miles of highway by my side. My journey would not have been the same without him.

This has been a project in trust. Trust in my inner vision, my instincts, my new friends, and trust in a belief that life is good and only gets better. Trusting the horses I have ridden. Trusting Star to be in a grand ranch house one minute and a barn the next, and to know the difference. I set out on this adventure to find my soul, and I filled my heart. My life will never be the same again.

The people of this book have given me a new look at myself through their love and their lives. The new friendships and extended families have grown beyond my wildest dreams. They invited me into their homes and hearts, sharing hugs, laughs, tragedy, and philosophy, teaching me and showing me by their example to grow beyond my hesitations. I am more complete, and I thank them. I rediscovered the strength of simple values like kindness, courtesy, graciousness, commitment, appreciation, compassion, gratitude, and love. I have searched my heart to find a way to thank these people. The best I can offer is to celebrate their lives through my photography and this book.

Star
positioning for a better view of
livestock work in Colorado

HOW IT ALL BEGAN

D A V I D   D A R Y

As a boy growing up in Kansas during the late 1940s, I usually spent Saturday afternoons at a local movie house. Admission was only twelve cents, and those few pennies provided more than two hours of escape from school work or the summer heat. There would be an adventure serial, cartoon, newsreel, and two feature films that almost always included a Western. My friends and I called them cowboy shows, and they were the chief attraction for us. Today they provide fond memories of youth, but the Westerns created impressions in my young mind that took years to correct. One of those notions was that cattle ranching was born in the American West; this was not the case.

American cattle ranching began with the Spanish nearly five hundred years ago, when Christopher Columbus returned to the New World for a second time. He set anchor off the north coast of Hispaniola near present Cape Haitien, Haiti, on January 2, 1494, and unloaded twenty-four stallions, ten mares, and an unknown number of cattle. They were the first such creatures in the Western Hemisphere.

The cattle and the horses prospered on Hispaniola. Beginning in 1498, small cattle ranches, or royal villas, were established to increase the supply of breeding stock. By the early 1500s, as the Spaniards settled modern-day Puerto Rico, Jamaica, Cuba, and other islands in the West Indies, the practice of stock raising was extended to each of the new settlements. The availability of cattle delighted the Spaniards,

Sparrowk
Livestock cowboys working cattle on the Mee Ranch, King City, California

who had an aversion to the beefless diet of the natives.

As the Spanish became firmly entrenched in the West Indies early in the sixteenth century, Hernán Cortés set out to conquer New Spain. Even before he captured what is today Mexico City and conquered the Aztecs, several head of cattle—one account says they were all calves—were landed on the banks of the Panuco River near present-day Tampico. These apparently were the first cattle in what is now Mexico. In less than a year Spanish settlers, supplies, and an increasing number of cattle and horses arrived in New Spain.

Cortés was one of the first Spaniards to realize that Mexico's greatly varied topography and climate were ideally suited to raising stock. When the promise of unlimited supplies of gold was not fulfilled, Cortés turned his attention to raising stock in the lush valley of Mexicalzimgo, more than 8,500 feet above sea level. This beautiful valley, south of modern Toluca, became the chief center of experimentation in cattle breeding. The grasslands were stocked with cattle, which soon multiplied, and it was here that cattle ranching was born in the Western Hemisphere.

Other Spaniards soon followed Cortés's example and began to graze cattle on land south and west of Mexico City. Within a few years cattle became plentiful there and eastward to the grass-covered plains and valleys near Perote and Tepeaca. The Spaniards let their animals wander at will, but Indian farmers soon began complaining about trampled fields of maize and other crops. They demanded that cattle should not go unattended while crops were in the fields. Although the crown had insisted that the rights of Indians were to be respected, large numbers were driven from their lands,

leaving the Spaniards quarreling over property and disputing ownership of cattle, many of which were not branded. It became commonplace for a Spaniard to claim all unbranded strays and to brand them as his own. Centuries later this practice would be called "mavericking," first in Texas, then elsewhere in the American West.

In an effort to resolve such problems and keep peace among Spaniards and between Spaniards and Indians, the town council of Mexico City, which was composed of several cattle raisers, ordered the establishment of a local stockmen's organization called the Mesta. Established on June 16, 1529, it was patterned after a similar institution in Old Spain. The Mesta was to become the granddaddy of all organized stockmen's groups in the Western Hemisphere.

The town council ordered that "there shall be two judges of the Mesta in the city who shall, twice annually, call together all stockmen who should make it known if they had any stray animals in their herds." The town council further directed each stock owner to have his own brand, which would be used in the future to identify all his animals. Stock owners were then directed to register their brands in what undoubtedly was the first brand book in the Western Hemisphere, kept at Mexico City. Later, the use of such brand books as a public record of all registered brands would spread northward and throughout the American West.

Early in the 1530s, a number of Spaniards appropriated grazing land to the west and northwest of Mexico City. As they established their cattle herds in what is today southern Queretaro, northern Michoacan, and southern Guanajuato, disputes erupted between Indian farmers, who

claimed much of the land, and the cattle ranchers, who, in typical conquistador fashion, had taken it without asking. To solve the problems the crown in 1533—soon after New Spain was officially proclaimed a Spanish colony—established common grazing lands for livestock owned by Spaniards as well as Indians. The concept of open-range ranching was born in the Western Hemisphere.

From the first arrival of the conquistadors in New Spain, the horse had given the Spaniards superiority over the Indians. Perhaps fearing that Indians on horseback would be formidable antagonists, Spanish colonial law prohibited Indians from owning or riding horses. But gradually, as the cattle population increased, this changed. With so many cattle on the common grazing ranges, rustling increased, and it became necessary to stand watch over one's cattle. Most Spaniards viewed such work with disdain. Even the mission padres, with their own herds of cattle, had similar feelings.

These men of God, many of whom did not like to ride horses, viewed the handling of cattle as menial work, and it appears that the padres were the first to find a solution to the problem: they chose to teach their new converts—Indians, Negroes, and other non-Spaniards—to ride horses and to look after cattle. Gradually the vaquero—the cowboy—was born.

When the Spaniards discovered rich silver deposits at Zacatecas in 1546 and hurriedly moved into the frontier region of New Spain, the demand for beef in the mining camps and new settlements became great. Ranchers drove cattle into the region to take advantage of high prices paid for beef—a pattern that would be repeated in the nineteenth century far to the north, when American cattlemen drove cattle half a continent away to capitalize on premium prices paid by hungry gold miners in California and, later, in the gold fields of what is now Colorado, and still later to the railhead cattletowns of Kansas.

Open-range
grazing, Highway 50, Nevada

A cowboy
slowly moves Double J. A. Land &
Livestock cattle toward the gate,
Bridgeport, California.

By the 1550s, wild cattle were so plentiful in New Spain that it was not uncommon for a calf not to see a human being until the animal was full-grown or even several years old. The wild temperament of these animals made them so difficult to handle that ranchers began to round them up regularly so they could become accustomed to men. This regular activity began during the 1550s and became known as the *rodeo*, from the Spanish *rodear*, meaning "to go around" or "to surround or encircle." The rodeo was simply a roundup that may have been inspired by a form of Indian hunt; it was nothing like its modern-day cousin in the American West.

By the end of the sixteenth century, cattle ranching was firmly established in the New World, but economic and political problems brought change as the seventeenth century began. The mining boom in New Spain had collapsed, and Spain itself faced retrenchment of colonial enterprises because of the depletion of its financial reserves. In an effort to raise capital, the crown offered to sell wealthy ranchers and other landowners full title to the land they occupied—including those who had seized land years before without any official sanction. Soon ranchers were marking their land boundaries, and their ranches or *haciendas* grew in importance. Each *hacendado*, or hacienda owner, became something of a lord, creating a world to his own liking.

One marvels at what the Spanish accomplished in cattle ranching during their first century in New Spain, but then the

to watch the herds. When mission herds increased in the 1770s, the crown began providing the padres enormous tracts of grazing land. By 1800 the mission fathers had a monopoly on cattle ranching in California, and since cattle raising was the only industry in the region, the padres controlled the region's economy. Then, between 1786 and the early 1820s, the crown made about twenty private land grants. Not all of these private ranchos were used for cattle ranching, nor did those who did raise cattle make a dent in the mission-controlled economy. But the foundation had been set, and about a decade after Mexico declared independence from Spain in 1821, as the mission system faded, California entered upon its era of large private ranchos.

The California ranches were, in many ways, like the haciendas that still flourished in northern regions of Old Mexico. The homage paid the rancho owners—they were called *rancheros*—was similar to that accorded the hacendado in Mexico or a medieval lord in Europe. As their holdings grew, the rancheros recruited large numbers of Indians from the rapidly decaying mission settlements to work as vaqueros. Whether a ranchero lived on his rancho or not, it became the custom to leave its management in the hands of a *mayordomo*, who made certain that the cattle were cared for and that other labors were performed. Each California rancho was virtually self-sustaining, except for the luxuries obtained from Yankee trading vessels stopping along the coast to trade for cattle hides and tallow. The wives and families of the rancheros usually lived in much comfort.

The mission system that had worked so well in Spanish California was not successful in Spanish Texas. Although more than fifty missions were established there

land favored stock raising, especially in northern regions, and the people adapted to the land. Similar favorable conditions were found in many areas of what is today the American Southwest—Arizona, New Mexico, and Texas. But cattle ranching in these areas did not grow at the same pace that it had to the south during the first hundred years following the Spanish conquest. The cattle prospered, but New Spain lacked the population and resources necessary for the development of the northern frontier region. Thus, during the eighteenth century, Spaniards turned to the mission system in an attempt to make Spanish colonists out of native Indians.

The system worked in what is today California, where twenty-one missions were established from San Diego to Sonoma. Nearly all of the missions engaged in cattle ranching, using Indian converts—on foot—

during the Spanish reign—twenty were active in Texas even before the first California mission was established at San Diego—the crown failed to support them after Spain acquired Louisiana in 1761. Indeed, few Spaniards settled in Texas. The padres failed to convert most of the Texas Indians, and by the late 1700s many Texas missions had been abandoned, some destroyed by Indians.

American colonists began to settle in Texas about the time Mexico declared its independence from Spain in 1821. But cattle ranching as it was then known on the haciendas of south and southwest Texas, across the Rio Grande to the south, and far to the west on the ranchos of California, was not practiced by the Americans. Even the word *ranching* was foreign to their language, having come from the word *ranch*, which in turn was derived from the Spanish word *rancho*, meaning "farm," particularly one devoted to the breeding and raising of livestock. In the area of the eastern United States, where the first cattle had arrived at Jamestown, Virginia, in 1611, stock raising was usually conducted along with farming and on a relatively small scale, except in a

Russ Ranch at Cape Mendocino, California, the westernmost cattle-grazing land in the continental United States

few southern states. Only in the South was stock normally herded on horseback; in the North, men and boys worked on foot. The adoption of Spanish-style cattle ranching was gradual, since the farmer's purpose in raising cattle was to provide beef for himself and his family.

By the 1830s, however, many American settlers in Texas were beginning to raise large numbers of cattle. They learned how to handle the animals by observing the Mexican vaqueros at work. The Texas cowboy borrowed many of the tools and techniques of the vaquero, and, as the Texas frontier pushed westward after the Texas revolution in 1836, Texans began adopting the Mexican open-range approach to cattle raising as well. Although it is impossible to say in what year the range-herding technique was first used by Anglo-Texans, it was in evidence in most regions by the late 1840s.

Finding markets for their stock was often difficult for the Texas ranchers. Some cattle were driven to Louisiana river towns like Shreveport and New Orleans, where they were sold. By the late 1840s, some were being shipped on steamers from Texas to New Orleans and other markets along the Gulf Coast, though most Texas cattle seem to have been driven overland. The same was true in California following the discovery of gold in 1848. The surge of gold seekers created a demand for beef in and around the mining fields. California rancheros soon were driving their cattle to the new mining settlements and selling them at great profit. During the early 1850s cattle were being driven from Missouri and Texas to California. As long cattle drives became more commonplace, a few men drove cattle from Texas to Missouri and Illinois. There is at least one case where cattle were driven in 1854 from Texas to Indiana and then shipped to New York City by rail. Texas ranchers were searching out markets for the ever-increasing number of cattle.

During the Civil War many Texas cattle were driven east to provide beef for Confederate soldiers. Still others were driven to Mexico and sold, but, like the times, the markets were not good. Many cattle ranch-

Sombrero
Ranch horse drive on a highway in western Colorado

Double J. A.
Land and Livestock Co. drive cattle
through the town of Smith,
Nevada.

Lacey & Son
Ranches moving cattle from winter
range in Olancha, California, onto
summer range in the southern Sierra
Nevada

Circle Bar
Ranch homestead: one of the oldest
sod-roof log cabins in Wyoming

ers went off to fight, leaving boys and old men to watch the cattle. Few bulls were castrated, the animals increased in number, and many became wild, wandering the open ranges—especially after winter storms in 1863 and 1864. When the war ended in 1865, the returning Texans found countless cattle and turned to ranching to make a living. Land was easy to acquire; unlike other states, Texas had been able to retain its public land when it joined the Union. Men unable to purchase land simply took over an unclaimed area or settled for a 160-acre homestead—preferably near rivers, streams, or good springs. You did not need to *own* much land to be a cattle rancher in Texas following the Civil War, since all public land was generally viewed as open range. A rancher would build his head-quarters, consisting of a frame house to live in, one or more corrals for saddle horses, and other small frame buildings as needed. In areas of southwest Texas and along the Mexican border, many ranch houses and corrals were constructed of adobe.

Ranchers engaged in what were called "cow hunts" in an effort to gather and brand the wild cattle. Cow hunts had existed in Texas during the 1840s and 1850s, but by 1870 they were called roundups, a word still used today. Unlike most ranching terms in Texas, which can be traced to a Spanish-Mexican origin, the word *roundup* first appeared in the mountain country where North Carolina, Kentucky, Tennessee, and the two Virginias meet. In that region Americans let their cattle run at large. Once a year they would "round up" their stock, brand the calves, and remove any cattle to be sold or slaughtered for meat.

The chuck wagon was another American innovation, which appeared in Texas ranching between 1865 and 1870. On cow hunts lasting only a few days, cowboys and vaqueros had carried their own rations. On longer hunts, pack mules or horses might carry the supplies of roasted coffee, bacon, and hard biscuits. But Texans involved in

Cattle drive through a sixteen-mile snow trench at the Big Horn Ranch, Cowdrey, Colorado

really long drives to California or to Missouri and Kansas Territory during the 1850s carried their supplies in ox-drawn carts or in wagons. As ranching pushed onto the Texas plains following the Civil War, mess wagons—or "chuck wagons," as they became known—appeared. Most historians agree that Charles Goodnight, the first rancher to settle in the Texas panhandle, was the man responsible for the first customized chuck wagon constructed in 1866.

Another purely American innovation

was barbed wire, which appeared in the late 1870s. At first many ranchers shunned it. Open-range ranchers had little need for fences, aside from small corrals for their saddle horses. During the 1860s and 1870s, most Texas cattlemen thought the ranges would always be free and open, but gradually they came to realize that full ownership of the land was the only guarantee of complete control of the water and grass for their cattle. Barbed-wire fences soon came into use to control stock and to discourage

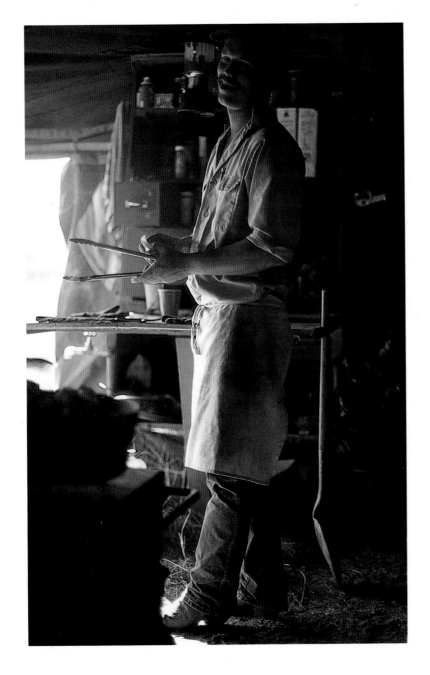

Lonny Vincent, chuck-wagon cook, Moorhouse Ranch

Moorhouse Ranch chuck wagon

trespassing. As ranchers sought to improve the quality of their cattle through breeding programs, confinement and control of stock became increasingly important, and the open-range system of cattle ranching was not conducive to control. By the 1880s, cattle ranching had spread northward from Texas, New Mexico, and Arizona into Montana and the Pacific Northwest. Cattlemen, including Theodore Roosevelt, who established two ranches in the Badlands of Dakota Territory, turned to using barbed wire. For many Easterners, Roosevelt made cattle ranching in the West fashionable during that decade.

Although no two nineteenth-century cattle ranchers were alike, many had similar traits. Most were self-reliant, had worked hard and understood the value of money, and most were very independent. Some—

like Captain Richard King and Abel Head "Shanghai" Pierce—were colorful characters. Many became wealthy and invested their profits in land, in more cattle, and in building and furnishing larger ranch houses and providing gracious living conditions for their families. The successful cattle ranchers were good businessmen, many attracting eastern capital for their enterprises. But many ranchers and investors were wiped out by the terrible winter storms of 1886–87. From Montana southward into Texas, thousands of cattle died.

The golden age of open-range ranching in America was gone as the twentieth century dawned. Herds of Texas longhorns no longer wound their way up the Sedalia, Chisholm, Western, or any of the other cattle trails to the often wild railhead cattle towns. These things were only memories.

The Vogler log
cabin on the Shaffer Ranch, Walden,
Colorado

Historic
building at the legendary King
Ranch, Kingsville, Texas

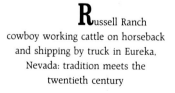

Like most modern cattle drives, the Double J. A. Land & Livestock drive uses highways instead of trails.

Russell Ranch cowboy working cattle on horseback and shipping by truck in Eureka, Nevada: tradition meets the twentieth century

Most ranchers owned or leased the land their cattle grazed. The lanky Texas longhorns had been replaced by more profitable kinds of cattle produced in careful breeding programs. And railroads shipped stock direct from ranching country.

Today, many traditional tools and techniques are still used on ranches to handle cattle. Cowboys may still be seen on their horses, and cattle roundups still occur. But airplanes, helicopters, pickup trucks, and all-terrain vehicles are often used in place of horses; two-way radios provide instant communication; trucks carrying prepared foods have replaced chuck wagons. Large semitrailer trucks now carry the cattle to market. Computers and other forms of modern technology have been mixed with the old ways to help ranchers make a profit. Still other changes will undoubtedly come to American cattle ranching, but constant reminders of its colorful and romantic past remain, its roots deeply embedded in the heritage of Spanish and Mexican ranching and that of early Texas and California. This past continues to shape the lives of many American ranchers and their families.

Oxbow Ranch cattle drive moving down the highway, Prairie City, Oregon

THE WEST OF TRUE MYTH

GRETEL EHRLICH

There's a fundamental need to move out from under small and severe tyrannies, political and economic ones as well as those we impose on ourselves. We have to eat and breathe; we have to make peace with ourselves. The western frontier was a physical answer to this need for space. It was a place to go to. Even now, when I stand on the hill by our house and look out over the Big Horn Basin, its breaks and draws and red-walled mesas, its strings of cottonwoods following creeks out of the mountains, I can see that this country still carries with it the possibility of a fresh start, of air, food, sanity.

When an eighty-year-old Hungarian violinist came to visit me one summer she stepped off the train, dressed like a char-acter out of *Anna Karenina*, and said, "Ahhh . . . all this space . . . all this great breathing!" Even now, in a world sadly characterized as a place of diminishing returns, open space is seen as a mythic zone essential to life itself.

The myths of the West have been par-ented and nurtured by ideas of freedom, real and imagined, urgent and neurotic. When we start any new project in life— a new ranch, a marriage, a novel—we come to it with the best intentions and inspirations, but along with fierce energy and spontaneity comes so much cultural baggage, habitual patterns, and preconceptions, we realize that freedom is, itself, a myth.

When I asked a seventy-year-old rancher what he thought about the old days of the

Jack Sparrowk and cowboy crew working cattle in preparation to ship, Mee Ranch, King City, California

West he said, "Hell, it's all been one big myth." His wife, "Mike," who has cowboyed all her life, replied, "Myths? Damn it, they're all true. They just didn't tell *everything*."

There are, of course, two meanings to the word *myth.* A myth can be a false idea, a stereotype, an unrealized hope, a lie; or it can be a deep-rooted bare-root narrative risen from what Thomas Mann called "The bottomless well of the past" and that helps us reconcile to the predicament of existence.

Joseph Campbell defines mythology as "a function of biology, a production of the human imagination which is moved by the energies of the organs of the body operating against each other." In other words, myths aren't fabrications of the chamber of commerce. They arise from reactions to physical stimuli. They evolve organically and grow like a vine from compost into images and words, feeling their way into a culture. No better definition of myth could be applied to Westerners, since what we understand about where we are and who we are comes to us first in a blunt, physical way: through the freezing and thawing of the ground as well as through our hands and toes; through

the birth cramps and death gasps of animals; through the soreness and ecstasies of our bodies, worn out from fourteen-hour days in the saddle and another five in the dance hall. It's through our cracked and bleeding lips, chapped from wind, that we first articulate what we have felt and seen.

Myths are acts of interpretation, of aspiration, not analysis. They can be as lyrical, grizzly, thronged, and revelatory as any summer lightning storm. They are the bright signposts inside us that describe the deep correspondence between ourselves and nature and prescribe a course of human conduct in context of this tryst. We hurl up the raw elements of life—a blizzard, a colony of ants, a death in the family, the repetition of seasons—and myths that grow from these give back a world that is, in every tiny aspect, sacred. Myths are the stories we tell about how meaning comes into our lives.

The first West was west of here, in southern California and on the borderlands of Arizona, New Mexico, and Texas. After Cortés's nightmarish conquest of Aztec Mexico, the Spaniards moved north, up the coast of California, desecrating aboriginal settlements as they went, and eventually established huge ranchos where cattle and horse herds ran loose and multiplied. So much of what we think of as western comes from the Mexicans: chaps, spurs, hacka-mores, silver bits, western saddles, ropes, and dally roping—though instead of roping steers, they caught grizzly bears for fun. Horsemanship, a passion for horseflesh, and all the recklessness and bravado that goes with it came from them, as did the word *ranch* and the sense of a ranch as an expansive, generous, self-sufficient community—a small empire, complete with vineyards, chapels, capacious kitchens, and clusters of adobes to house all who worked there.

From the other direction—from the East Coast of this continent—came the Northern Europeans. No group of people could have been more opposite, and along with their fastidious Puritan ways came a germ of fear, a feeling that these open spaces doled out death as often as they gave life.

So the Rocky Mountain West was a meeting place for very different kinds of people. I like to think of the Continental Divide as a long, beautiful, trembling spine, this highest ground of our country, toward which cultures from divergent points of the compass were magnetized—where exuberance and fastidiousness, energy and carelessness, generosity and greed, morality and lawlessness tumbled together in a lively, mongrel salad of contradictions.

There was a further complication in all this crashing of cultures: the so-called New World to which these people had migrated was, of course, new only to them, having been inhabited continuously for ten thousand years by Native Americans. Not only did the settlers find the landscape here difficult, even insulting, but the aboriginal cultures they were forced to confront were so complex in spiritual and social ways as to be incomprehensible to many who came here. Even before they got their horses picketed and their wagons unloaded, some realized that the myth of freedom had become chimerical. They had been naive to think that a place was theirs for the taking; they failed to understand that the first act of freedom occurs inside ourselves and entails letting go of who we think we are and where we think we are. It is an internal unburdening, a willingness to see what is actually here.

The first Europeans to come through the West were explorers and trappers. They were deeply eccentric men with an aboriginal knack for survival. They didn't come here to stay, as later settlers did; they came to see, to make a little money, to follow the game trails, ridges, and drainages, to live day by day. Space implied movement. If they didn't always know exactly where they were, they could at least read the lay of the land and understood how geography worked. Nor did they go undaunted by northern winters: if they didn't stick around for them, it wasn't because they weren't tough—they were just smarter than we are.

Soon the serious influx of settlers began, encouraged by a series of land reform and homestead acts—the Homestead Act of 1862, which included a land bonus for Civil War veterans, the Desert Land Act of 1877, and the Kincaide Home Act of 1909—which doled out virtually free but meager portions of land to those who could improve upon it.

From the South, youngsters signed on with the trail herds moving north from Texas or east from Oregon and California. These great movements of livestock toward unfenced grasslands represented a rite of passage not only for the cattle but for the young men who rode. Such a job was a traveling scholarship—the Harvard of cowboying, but with bigger stakes: it was easy to lose your life during the river crossings, to bog down in quicksand or get trampled by a stampede, but if you made it, you were paid, and you had endured.

The ranchers who received these herds had amassed great chunks of land along the creeks and rivers of these states and essentially laid claim to the public grazing lands. Open space was a currency to them— a terrestrial bank account from which they

Enroute to summer range, Lacey & Son Ranch cattle are gathered in a mountain meadow.

spent freely. The well-to-do built palatial houses: visual emblems of the notion that they were masters of nature and land. They overstocked the range, and when the winter of 1886 hit, they learned that to think of oneself as a master of nature is really to become its slave.

Meanwhile, on the east-west trails, there was bumper-to-bumper traffic. With the homesteaders came the Jeffersonian logic of the grid: of order imposed on chaos, of limits placed on the wildness inside each of us. With the congestion came further impeachments of freedom: barbed wire abrogated space; the class, religious, and racial conflicts any of us would be glad to flee from took root here. If any new beginnings were to be made, they had to originate in the heart and rise from the same old battles fought everywhere.

Not everyone who ended up here intended to stay. A friend's grandfather was trying to take a herd of cattle from Nevada to their home place in Nebraska when a winter storm hit. He happened to be on the Green River, and when spring came and he saw the luxurious grass coming up, he stayed, founding the town of Big Piney, Wyoming, where his grandchildren still ranch today.

The Mormons were dispatched by Brigham Young to settle some of the less desirable land in the Rocky Mountain states. The history of the Big Horn Basin where I live is the history of finding water. The 20,000 acres the Mormons claimed here

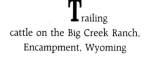

Trailing
cattle on the Big Creek Ranch,
Encampment, Wyoming

were barren and waterless. One friend's family arrived in October with thirteen children, a bag of apple seeds, and fourteen sheep. For the first year, they slept in tents on the Shoshone River. The second year all able-bodied men were enlisted to dig by hand what would be called the Sidon Canal. Still in use today, it is thirty-seven miles long, twenty-seven feet across, and sixteen feet deep. The project took four years. Along the way a huge boulder gave them trouble: it couldn't be moved. As a last resort, the men held hands around the rock and prayed. The next morning, it is said, the boulder rolled out of the way. With the completion of the canal, the Mormons built a church

and a school and drew for town lots where houses would be built communally. "It was a socialistic sonofabitch from the very beginning," my friend Frank likes to say. "It was a beautiful damned thing. These 'rugged individualists' forget how things got done around here, and not so damned many years ago at that."

While the Mormons clustered in small towns, other groups of settlers—many from southern states—homesteaded the foothills of the Big Horn Mountains. When one man went out to kill a deer because they had run out of food, he was stranded by a fall storm. After waiting four days for his return, his wife started walking toward the tiny

Corrals on the historic Sun Ranch at Devil's Gate— the split in the rocks—on the Sweetwater River, Wyoming

L͟acey & Son
Ranch cattle drive from desert
winter range to summer range in
the southern Sierra Nevada
Mountains

had been. They used space in a political way: because there was usually a posse after them, they were careful to stay a day's ride ahead, resting just over a county or state line, outside that sheriff's jurisdiction. Though they were at odds with society, they had made peace with the rugged terrain. Space equaled time: they traveled at night, and they traveled light. They had the wonderful advantage of privacy, which we've lost since the advent of helicopters. They could hide a herd of stolen horses in a steep canyon for a day or a winter without being found.

If total liberation was missing from the westward experience, there were still ways in which people could make a place for themselves, and there was a sense that our destinies are somehow maleable. As one rancher who settled in the Shell Valley said, "Isn't it a great thing to have had a hand in the evolution of a society?"

Despite the easy-going friendliness and hospitality of Americans, I think we are a people prone to loneliness because of the vast and desolate landscape we've inherited and the antisocial environments we've built for ourselves. We could have learned more about architecture from the Mexicans, but we didn't. In the West, it is our solitude that unites us. The farther apart we are in miles, the closer we feel. A frontier does away with the oppressive idea of perfection: our neighbors aren't always our choicest friends, and our towns often seem to lack almost everything. Living well here a hundred years ago and today—for those of us who live on ranches—is the art of making do. It is a democratizing process. So much in American life has had a corrupting influence on our requirements for social order. Traditionally, ranch life and the Native American societies here have stood for the

settlement of Kane at the foot of the mountains. She was pregnant and had gone into labor. She had the child somewhere on the mountain during the night. It was born dead. She walked on into Kane, badly snowblinded and bleeding. A week later they found her husband's body fifty yards from the house.

Besides the social injustices people encountered when they came here, there was the injustice of weather.

Cowboys on the lam and hard-core rustlers made use of the western landscape in a different way: they traveled in groups and often lived in caves. A few summers ago I hiked down to the Hole-in-the-Wall Cave. I could still see where the bunkbeds had been lashed to posts with rawhide straps and where the gang's cooking fire

achievements of man and nature, man and animal, not the machine. I think this still holds true—if not always in practice, then at least as a sustaining value.

Big ranches are miniature societies. It seems there is room enough for everyone on them. The big sheep outfit where I lived when I first came here hired a crew of a hundred men and women during lambing. Among them was a town idiot, a syphilitic recluse whom we found one day shaking his finger at the badly decayed carcass of a cow and saying, "Now I don't want you to do that ever again!" There was a fast-talking cowgirl who'd had eight children and three husbands and kept two shotguns above her bed; a handful of alcoholics, one of whom was hit by a car because he was on his hands and knees by the side of the road barking at cars like a dog. There were two WW II vets with metal plates in their heads and a nagging case of the shakes, and a pig farmer who would rather have been a singer who said to me when I met him, "Sweet-

Predawn breakfast and coffee at the Sombrero Ranch during the fall horse drive; horses will be moved fifty miles to winter range at Browns Park, Colorado

Sombrero
Ranch horse drive along a
Colorado highway

Roadside
break, Sombrero Ranch horse drive

heart, when you're lookin' at me, you're lookin' at country."

Neighborliness is a prerequisite for ranch life. It is a moral imperative. The cowboy stands for a sense of community: a herd of animals and a ranch full of people on whom he is dependent and who are dependent on him. Those boys who rode north on the trail drives learned that cowboying requires impeccable teamwork. The image of a hired hand riding off alone in the sunset is more likely a cowboy who has just lost his job. Neighbors always did and still do help each other during brandings and gatherings, calving and lambing, or when the pipes freeze up, when children are sick, when sheepherders quit, or when someone doesn't get home from checking fence or riding a colt. There is a fine thread that links us together, a network of relatedness. What we see is not the "I" of the individualist, but a collective "I."

The myth of the American cowboy is a stale idea, made mock-serious by Marlboro ads, used by one recent American president to supplant the lack of depth and direction in some of his own actions and ideas. Heroism has been mistakenly aligned with tough-mindedness, even violence at the expense of others, yet the heroic nature of a cowboy's or rancher's life has nothing to do with brute force. If they "take a deep seat" in the saddle, it's because they've just gotten bucked off two or three times and are trying desperately to stay on; if they look gruff, it's because their lips are too chapped to permit a smile, or else they've just survived another unexpected blast of violent weather. It's nature that's violent, not the cowboy. His life is spent ducking and dodging, and surviving various storms.

Ranchers are inextricably linked to

family, family in the largest sense of the word. It doesn't mean they necessarily have spouses or children, but that their work is wholly taken up by breeding, birthing, nurturing. They're providers and protectors; they live and die within the large communities of animals, plants, humans, and while some of them may be alcoholic, misfit, lying sons of bitches, their very desperation and need has driven them to hook up with the tolerant society a ranch can provide. True heroism, then, is simply a life dictated by the heart, pushing far out into recklessness, tenderness, humor, and whim.

The first Wyoming ranch I lived on employed thirteen to fifteen sheepherders. Except for one couple, they lived alone. When I started riding out to visit them, I was referred to as "that girl-bachelor," and it was our mutual aloneness and, sometimes, loneliness that cemented our bond. Eccentrics, social outcasts, minor- and major-league alcoholics, they had given up on

A yearling "baby" bums a treat from rancher Cebe Hanson, Big Horn Ranch, Cowdrey, Colorado

the conventions of society and lived a long way from town, from family, from sexual nourishment. "Me and my dog, that's all I have," one herder told me, then chased me around a huge outcrop of granite, trying to get me "bedded down." Usually our encounters were more agreeable. They cooked for me, entertained me with stories of their lives, rode with me at least halfway home— for "meeting halfway" is one canon of range etiquette.

Subject to extravagant flights of delusion and fantasy, the herder, alone for much of his life, too often succumbs to self-hate. There's nothing to bolster his sense of self; there's no give and take, no exchange of oxygen. The air deadens. Nature's violent strokes leave scars that confirm one's insignificance—yet heroism endures. Resourceful, keenly observant, he is an expert on loneliness and patience, his life a living definition of those words.

If men in the West have been wrongly stereotyped, then women haven't been mentioned at all. Yet, on many ranges and ranches, they are the strong ligament on which the workings of the ranch flex and bend. On the ranches where I've lived, the women didn't stay inside and cook. They rode behind cattle, roped and pulled calves, cut out replacement heifers in the fall, culled cows. They kept the books, went to talk to the bankers to renew their operational loans, as well as cooked, cleaned, and helped their children navigate their lives. These were family ranches, small enough to be run by a couple with one or two hired hands (often women, too). This was no feminist paradise; it was simply that a few ranches used all the help they could get. Gender didn't matter. Ranchers who had only daughters raised their kids to be good hands, and these women raised *their* children the same way—a simple transmission of skills.

Mary Frances Tisdale Hinckeley, called "Mike," taught me to handle cattle and rope. The second day I moved to the town of Shell, she called and asked if I wanted to ride. By riding she didn't mean trotting up the road for pleasure, but putting in fourteen-hour days for no pay. I accepted ecstatically, and from then on we worked as a team. Over the mountain we'd go, hauling six head of horses to the Wolf Mountains in Montana to ride for two weeks, gathering several thousand head of steers and mother cows. We had car troubles and flat tires, we were bucked with and fallen on by our various mounts, we spent sleepless nights

Dickinson family and friends building a corral on their Rife Ranch in southwestern Wyoming

Russell Ranch
sheep band trailing north in eastern
Nevada

at the bars in Hardin, or outside watching the northern lights. Though I was without many cowboying skills, she would not let me hang back, so I worked the sorting corrals, roped at brandings, rode point (at the head of the herd) at high rates of speed down mountains just behind the lead cow or steer with five hundred or five thousand following closely behind.

Some days, four of us—Mike, Mary, Laura, and I—rode together. We'd gather the whole mountain, sort the heifer calves off from the steer calves at the weening corrals, then load the trucks and drive them down the mountain, come back and start all over again. "We have our widow-woman ways," Mary explained to an onlooker. "But we *do* get the work done, and because we take things a little slower, a little quieter

Kim Smith, Cottonwood Ranch cow boss, works cattle on the open range in northeastern Nevada.

Smith family and friends branding calves, Cottonwood Ranch, O'Neill Basin, Nevada

Leo Sommer
with daughter Jamie on Double J. A.
Land & Livestock cattle drive
through the mountains in California

John Ascuaga
and Jamie Sommer work the Double
J. A. Land & Livestock cattle drive,
which brings together friends and
family.

and easier, the cattle are the better for it, if you really want to know the truth.... But don't tell the men. They're kind of fragile, and they'd never understand."

The extended family of a ranching community includes men who work alone and women who hire out singly as cowboys, as well as husband-wife teams, sister-brother teams, or pairs of brothers who run the family ranch. It's not a glamorous life. Perhaps the notion of the antihero in American, European, and Japanese literature has risen as an effort to disavow the idea of "rugged individualism," of glamorousness. If cowboys perpetuate the myth of their lives—and this they do by telling larger-than-life stories about what's happened to them at the end of the week—then it's only the result of an aggravated loneliness, of physical frustrations and emotional inhibitions that need ventilation. It's not a hero's accolade they seek, but only a few laughs over a whiskey.

How do these Western myths function in our lives? What in them is instructive to us? Though we all feel a sadness that no uncharted land is left, no true wilderness, we've learned from the good and bad experiences of the frontier the meaning of freedom, heroism, wildness, and something about the processes of civilization. It's not the myths that are wrong, but our versions of reality. From the open space still surrounding us, we learn spiritual equivalents: that personal liberation is a kind of psychic space that represents clear-headedness and an ability to act without fraudulence. From the cowboy myths we learn that heroism isn't power play, but an act of submission— a communion of the human and the natural. The Western code reminds us to behave, to be disciplined, to be good neighbors; it teaches us the basics of compassion. From the inclemencies of weather we learn humor and humility, how to be coresidents, not conquerors, in the world.

Gathering cattle into a holding pasture for the next day's drive from the mountains to the home ranch, Oxbow Ranch, Prairie City, Oregon

THE COWBOY

JOHN R. ERICKSON

I'm in my forties now. My old Heiser saddle is hanging by a rope from a rafter in the garage. The spurs my Grampy Buck Curry made on a coal forge back in the Depression years, and which I wore almost every day for eight years, now hang on a coat rack in my office, beside my chaps and two catch ropes and straw hat that once belonged to Ace Reid's father.

I don't get too many opportunities to use them any more, maybe two or three times a year, when I go out and help old friends at roundup time.

I retired from full-time cowboying in July of 1981, but the instincts remain. I still read the "Help Wanted" ads in the *Livestock Weekly* every Saturday afternoon. I still study the condition of the grass when I drive down the highway, and when cattle are grazing close to the road, I find myself checking their ears and eyes and looking for sick ones.

It's hard for me to drive past a group of horses without going into the ditch, because my gaze lingers on them. I can see at a glance that most of them are idle and need riding, and I think to myself, "Boys, it's too bad we can't get together, because I've got the same problem. We'd both be better with more riding."

And when I happen upon a group of cowboys riding close to the highway, their hats pulled down to the tops of their ears, the collars of their coats turned up, their breath making fog in the air, their horses dancing and bursting with energy, Lord, I have to slow down and pull over to the

Del Nicewonger, manager, Mee Ranch, King City, California

The cowboy has been defined as "a hired hand on horseback" and as "merely folks, just a plain everyday bowlegged human." Those definitions are pretty good, although the second one is slightly dated. Fifty years ago, most cowboys might have been bowlegged, but today they're not. Why? Better nutrition and less time spent in the saddle, I would guess.

My own definition, if I were pressed to give one, would be that a cowboy is a common laborer with heroic tendencies and a sense of humor, who lives with animals.

There are four parts to that definition. Let's take them one at a time.

The cowboy is a common laborer. There may be some confusion in the public's mind about the difference between a cowboy and a rancher. This book has a separate chapter for each, and that's as it should be, because even though they often wear the same brand of clothes and drink from the same cup and look just about the same from a distance, they're not the same. They're quite different, in fact.

A rancher owns grassland upon which livestock graze, and he provides the management for the ranching operation. He makes the decisions on when to buy and sell. He hires employees and signs the paychecks. The laborers he hires to care for his livestock are cowboys.

Cowboying is a trade, much like carpentry or plumbing, and those who pursue it for a living have mastered certain skills. Just as you would expect a carpenter to be proficient in his use of the tape measure, level, square, hammer, and saw, so you would expect a cowboy to be a good horseman, windmill mechanic, and fence builder, and at least a fair roper, amateur veterinarian, welder, and stock-trailer mechanic.

Cowboys work for ranchers, not vice

side of the road and watch them for a few minutes, remembering when I was one of them.

I have been many things in my life— a farmhand, a bartender, a chaplain's assistant in a Boston hospital, a university student, a village handyman, and an author—but I was never prouder of who I was and what I did than when I made my living as a ranch cowboy.

When you use the term *cowboy* these days, you have to be careful. It's gotten a lot of mileage in recent years. We've had Hollywood cowboys and rodeo cowboys, rhinestone cowboys and Coca-cola cowboys, urban cowboys and midnight cowboys, Marlboro cowboys and Dallas Cowboys.

The cowboy I'm talking about is the ranch cowboy, the guy who makes his living taking care of cattle. Some people think he became extinct forty or fifty years ago, but he didn't. He's still very much around on ranches from Florida to California, from Canada to Mexico.

Harly Guess,
rancher, Maybell, Colorado

Sombrero
Ranch cowboys moving horses,
Maybell, Colorado

versa. Some ranchers work beside their cowboys, and some don't.

Cowboys usually own very little, often nothing more than a pickup, a few horses, their saddle and rigging, and personal possessions. Ranchers own land, livestock, vehicles, equipment, and houses.

Cowboys come and go. Ranchers remain in one spot and, oftentimes, are the third, fourth, or fifth generation to live on the ranch.

Ranchers belong to the middle class. Cowboys don't. Theirs is a notoriously low-paid profession that can't support a middle-class life-style. They don't really belong to any class. They're just cowboys. They usually associate with other cowboys, are indifferent to politics, and rarely belong to organizations in town.

Russell Ranch cowboy Terry Adams, Jr., Eureka, Nevada

Livestock truck driver waiting for cattle to be loaded, Eureka, Nevada

Ranchers are likely to be married and have a family. Cowboys—maybe and maybe not. Cowboying used to be a bachelor profession, because ranches lacked facilities for keeping wives and families. That isn't as true today as it used to be, and many outfits have replaced the bunkhouse, where bachelor cowboys slept together, with a tenant house, which is large enough to accommodate a cowboy and his family.

But being married to a cowboy and living in someone else's tenant house isn't an easy life for a woman, and many a cowboy has had to choose between his job and his marriage. If he chooses to save his marriage, as many young men do, he moves to town and finds a better-paying job. Chances are that his position will be filled by a younger man who is either single or who has pre-school-age children.

Cowboy, then, is a technical term. To say that you're one is to say that you're qualified to do certain tasks and use certain tools in a professional manner. In its original and strictest sense, cowboying has nothing to do with country-western music, rodeos, movies, saloons, gun fights, dancehall girls, or Marlboro cigarettes.

Cowboys have heroic tendencies. This is probably the most controversial part of the cowboy tradition. There are people in our society who seem to believe that heroes and heroism are things of the past, or that heroism never really existed in the first place. In recent years they have turned their guns on the cowboy and have tried to do a job on him.

But the heroism of the working cowboy isn't a joke. It isn't a put-on. It isn't something that has been cooked up by an advertising agency, and it isn't something that cheap minds will ever understand.

Cowboys are heroic because they exercise human courage on a daily basis. They live with danger. They take chances. They sweat, they bleed, they burn in the summer and freeze in the winter. They find out how much a mere human can do, and then they do a little more.

They reach beyond themselves.

Why does a man who is paid by the month stay up all night with a mare he doesn't own to help her shell out a foal he also won't own and that might kill him in two years when he climbs on its back for the first time?

Why does a man make the decision to skip his only day off and feed the cattle on

A Big Creek Ranch cowboy bottle feeds an orphaned calf, nearly frozen to death.

Working cattle in a snow storm, Cottonwood Ranch, Wells, Nevada

Cows do not always give birth easily. When a cow is having difficulty with a natural birth, she is rounded up and brought into the barn to be "pulled." Here, Bill Trampe and Don Rundell pull a calf (Trampe Ranches, Gunnison, Colorado). First they attach the chains to the front legs of the calf and adjust them. Next, they help the cow to dilate in order to accommodate the calf; the calf puller is in place, and they pull. First the head and shoulders come free, and then the calf emerges, alive and breathing.

Big Creek Ranch cowboy Ron Knodel pulls a calf (Encampment, Wyoming). He reaches in to put the chains on the front feet, and then starts to pull and position the calf. He adjusts the chain and hooks up the calf puller. After much effort, the front legs and head finally start to come; once the shoulders clear, the calf will emerge easily and is born live and healthy.

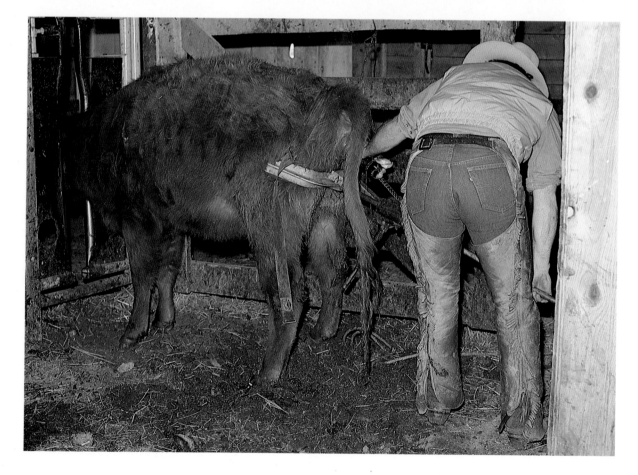

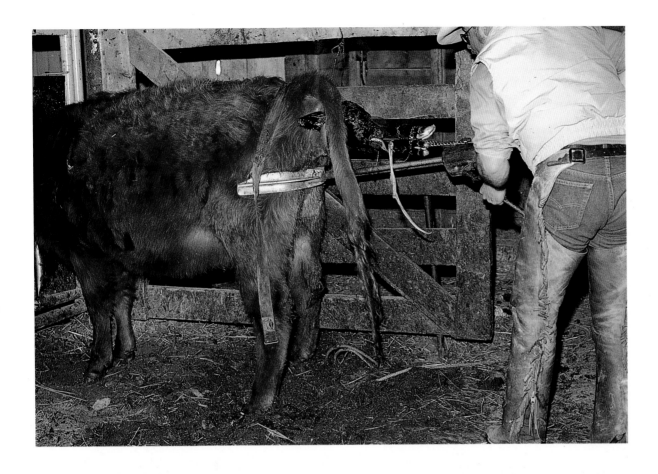

Taking a lunch
break during the Sombrero Ranch
horse drive

Moorhouse
cowboys fix "calf fries" after a day of
branding and castrating bull calves
in Hall County, Texas.

Sunday, when he knows the boss man wouldn't do it and he'll never be rewarded for it?

Why does a man risk his life roping a bull that has gone lame with foot-rot or fight a prairie fire or fix a windmill in a high wind or feed cattle in a blizzard?

The answers to those questions would have been obvious in simpler times: Because the man cares about something other than himself. Because he believes he's a part of a system that's more important than his own comfort. And because it's right to do it and wrong not to do it.

That's heroism on a small scale, and every cowboy I ever knew accepted it as part of his personal philosophy.

The cowboy has a sense of humor. Cowboys belong to one of the few groups in modern America that have retained a

strong oral tradition of storytelling. Telling stories has been part of the cowboy's pattern of life from the beginning, and it remains so today.

Cowboys generate good stories because they have stories to tell, based on personal experiences, and because they have managed to preserve the same kind of organic sense of humor that was found in the work of Mark Twain, Joel Chandler Harris, Charlie Chaplan, Laurel and Hardy, Will Rogers, Charlie Russell, and other great humorists of the past.

An "organic" sense of humor draws its inspiration from broad human tendencies and universal themes. It is gentle in tone and its intent is to entertain, perhaps even to teach a lesson, rather than to destroy. That sets it apart from satire and ridicule.

One doesn't often think of a sense of humor being an asset for survival, but it is. Cowboys have learned to use their sense of humor as a buffer between themselves and a world that is usually beyond their control, which might include nature's wrath, animals that don't respond to human reasoning, and a man's own stupid mistakes.

A friend of mine once climbed on a

big thoroughbred mare that had a history of blowing the cork. His companion, who was standing nearby, asked, "How long since you rode the old mare?"

Before the first cowboy could answer, the mare bogged her head and blew him right out of the stirrups. His head and feet swapped ends, and he stuck his nose into the ground. He sat up, shook the vapors out of his head, and said, "About three weeks."

Another fellow was driving back to the ranch late at night. On a country road, he fell asleep and crashed his pickup into a bridge. A bloody mess, he walked to the nearest neighbor's house and banged on the door.

The neighbor answered the knock and stared at his friend, whom he could hardly recognize. "My gosh, Joe, what happened!"

"Oh, my pickup quit on me."

Charles Goodnight, the first cattleman to enter the vast prairies of the Texas Panhandle, lived to a ripe old age but never joined a church. When he was in his nineties, his wife finally insisted that he do it. He was baptized in a stock pond near Happy, Texas.

Later, when a journalist asked what church he had joined, he said, "I don't know, but it's a damned good one."

One day in 1977 I stopped in to see a cowboy friend on a ranch in Oklahoma. His wife had gone to visit relatives and he had been batching for a week. I asked him how he was getting along.

With a sparkle in his eye, he said, "Not too bad, but the sink's got so full of dishes, I'm having to pee outside."

The cowboy's sense of humor helps him survive hard times and keep his place in the world in its proper perspective. In the hands of talented people, such as artist

The modern way to round up horses and check strays, Sombrero Ranch, Browns Park, Colorado

Moorhouse
Ranch cowboys work cattle against a
fence line and cut a cow out of the
herd, Hall County, Texas

Ace Reid and novelist Elmer Kelton, it is also a valuable natural resource that adds softness, humility, wisdom, and laughter to the jagged art forms of the modern age.

The cowboy lives with animals. There was a time when most Americans had some contact with livestock, but in the modern age that has become the exception rather than the rule. Today, most Americans do not see livestock outside of a zoo, nor do they participate in the system that brings food to their tables.

The relationship between livestock animals and their keepers is as old as civilization itself. It is a relationship that welds the lives of people and animals together in a common purpose—the survival and well-being of the animals and the people. It's not the same relationship that a city dweller might have with a poodle or a house cat, and it's hard for people who aren't involved with livestock to understand it. It doesn't involve love or caring in the conventional person-to-person sense, because the cowboy doesn't blur the distinctions between people and animals. To do so would deprive the animal of its identity and function and make it into a cartoon parody. From the cowboy's perspective, this would diminish both the man and the beast.

If you asked a cowboy if he loved his cattle and horses, he would probably deny it, even though his devotion to them might suggest that he does. He deals with them on a level where respect is the highest compliment. He respects cattle for their size and strength and cunning. He respects his horse for what it can do: its athletic ability, it's vision and sure feet, its intelligence, and its courage. Although we can't verify this with testimony, I believe that cattle and horses size up a man in exactly the same way and regard him either with respect or a lack of it. And if they don't respect him, he won't last long in the business.

Cowboys spend more time in the company of animals than they do with people. They live on animal time and order their lives by animal schedules. They feed animals and fight animals, help them come into the world and stand beside them when they leave it. This daily association can't help but affect the way cowboys view themselves and the world around them. One result of this is that cowboys sometimes appear to be more successful in their dealings with animals than with people. As the songs on the country music charts suggest, many a cowboy who can read a horse's mind has a terrible time understanding his girlfriend or wife.

Another result, this one more positive, is that animals have a way of improving people—slowing them down, making them more patient, giving them an opportunity to participate in the rhythms of nature. Human beings need the wisdom and companionship of livestock, and animals need the order, discipline, and sense of purpose we bring to them. We are improved through our contact with them, and they with us. So there is the cowboy as I have known him: a common laborer with heroic tendencies and a sense of humor, who lives with animals.

What about the so-called cowboy myth? Is there any substance to it?

If by myth we mean a kind of legitimate, non-scientific knowledge that can lead us to a deeper understanding of things, then yes, I say the cowboy myth is not only real, but it's an essential part of who we are as Americans.

We don't have knights or kings or gurus in our tradition, even though we might wish we did. We come from cowboys, and that's who we are, for better or for worse. The farther away we get from our cowboy heritage, the less we will know about who we are and how we fit into this vast universe we're still struggling to understand. I admit that I'm biased, but I don't think it would hurt this nation to hear more about the cowboy and less about crooked politicians, football players, and movie stars.

Loading up horses too weak to travel the fifty-mile horse drive, Browns Park, Colorado

Trimming the
hooves on range bulls, Big Horn
Ranch, Cowdrey, Colorado

Big Creek
Ranch cowboy Ron Knodel teaching
a calf to nurse, Encampment,
Wyoming

Several years ago, Willie Nelson recorded a song called "My Heroes Have Always Been Cowboys." Not long ago I was out working with a friend who began cowboying forty years ago. He mentioned that song and said, "You know, that's the way it's been for me. My heroes *have* always been cowboys, and I guess they still are."

I thought about that for a long time. I have two sons, ages thirteen and four, and I worry about the kind of world they're living in. If they decided to make heroes of some of the cowboys I've known, I'd be proud.

Settling the cattle and taking a break, Double J. A. Land & Livestock cattle drive in Nevada

HEROES OF
THE SADDLE

REUBEN ALBAUGH

Many reasons can be "bunched up" in the old tally book as to why the West is different and apart from the rest of this great world. The very topography of the rangeland, mountains, streams, forests, and plains that mothered the buffalo, wolf, prairie dog, and rattlesnake, typifies its uniqueness. Then, of course, you have the smell of sagebrush, the famous barbed wire, the windmill, the cow pony, and square dancing. It's the area that lies west of the 100th meridian.

But above all was the uniqueness of the cattlemen; each western community had its famous character. A cowman added more glamour and color to the land of the setting sun than everything else combined. His fame, courteous manner, his hospitality, his genuine friendliness, his way of entertaining, and his clever commentary were unlike those heard anywhere else on this planet. His integrity was beyond reproach; he could be trusted with uncounted gold; his handshake was a valid contract. He was readily accepted in all levels of society. There is a saying in the West, "If you can walk with kings and keep your common touch, you are a man." Cattlemen qualify. They wear the right brand.

They were known as a new breed in the West, businessmen on horseback. They left their indelible brand on western America, set its colorful outlook, its dress, its vocabulary, its traditions, and its style of living. They were described as rough and tough in the mountains, but always gentlemen in town. Leading cattle-

Bill Trampe working cattle, Trampe Ranches, Gunnison, Colorado

Jim Humphreys, Pitchfork Land & Cattle Co., and Dub Waldrip, Spade Ranches, share a story.

Togo and Lucille Moorhouse, Benjamin, Texas

Don Rundell doctoring a newborn calf, Trampe Ranches, Gunnison, Colorado
opposite

men were tall in the saddle yet poised in a tuxedo, whether entertaining at the Palace Hotel or brushing shoulders with presidents in Washington. They wore Stetson hats, cowboy boots, and jingling spurs, all symbols of their profession. They voted the conservative Republican ticket and adhered to the Teddy Roosevelt dictum, "Speak softly, but carry a big stick." Extremely independent, cattlemen still brag about standing on their own two feet and never asking for government assistance.

Cattle raising was never easy. Drought, market fluctuations, unpredictable financing, the Blue Northerns, stampedes, and blizzards could undo years of hard western toil. How the cattlemen coped with these hazards has produced many thrilling chapters of American history. The basis for many stories of the West has been cattle and cowmen. They go together. One cannot be mentioned without thinking of the other.

Although many Easterners considered the West young and the cattle business raw and wild, it should be remembered that raising cattle was well established many years before the British colony was founded at Jamestown. Next to fur trapping and mining, cattle raising is the oldest industry in our country, and the cowman is among the earliest American businessmen.

Although the cattleman of the West lived a reckless, slam-bang life, he was well mannered and his hospitality was the finest. A stranger was never asked questions and was always welcome at his camp to put up his horse and spear a bean. No one ever left a cattleman's ranch hungry. In cattle country a splendid wife, an outstanding horse, and a good dog were considered gifts of God.

The cattleman's life was not simple, as it dealt with cattle, grass, horses, and rain.

Cattle producers have many aphorisms that describe the weather: The frog that died before he had learned to swim; the cattle were guaranteed—never had been rained on. The best one is the prayer of cattleman and innkeeper of McArthur, California, Shird Eldridge: "Oh Lord, Dear Lord, give us water, a Chinook wind, and dishwater rain." When it came to weather, there was no place in this business for the weak or timid. The land they used was tough and hard, and offered no promises. Why did cattlemen remain in such a chancy business? Maybe because he did business from the back of a good cowhorse, and the outside of a horse is good for the inside of a man.

Cattlemen were known far and wide for their iron constitutions. They traveled light, carrying only a change of underwear, a bottle of whiskey, and silk handkerchiefs, always in a small black satchel. The cattleman's handkerchief was known as the "flag of the range." It wiped sweat from the brow, was used as a mask that kept dust out of the nose, tied around the neck to keep out the cold, and as a sling for a broken arm. Dressed up, the handkerchief became a necktie. When Jess Cornwell, cattleman of King City, California, was asked why he did not get a hotel room in Salinas for the Big Week Rodeo, he replied, "Who needs a room? The rodeo only lasts four days." Jess played poker all night and attended the show during the day so he had no time to sleep.

When on the range, a cattleman's meals consisted of biscuits baked in a Dutch oven, fried beef, water gravy, and dried fruit. The drink was usually strong black coffee, drunk "barefoot"—without cream or sugar. This "buckaroo coffee" was sometimes made by tossing a few handfuls of coffee in a pot of water and bringing it to a boil over a fire

John Ascuaga,
Double J. A. Land & Livestock

Horace Smith,
Cottonwood Ranch, O'Neill Basin,
Nevada

Neighboring
ranchers Roy Fulton and John Rice
discuss ranch news, Eureka,
California.

Evening meal
over an open campfire on a
Cottonwood Ranch pack trip into
the Jarbidge Wilderness Area,
Nevada

fornia skies, the mañana attitude was easily defended, and living was rich and carefree, as well as colorful and romantic.

So we entered the first chapter of the California cattle business in a blaze of glory so often captured in song and story.

The mission fathers were the first full-time cattlemen, who taught the Indians how to care for the livestock, to make butter and cheese, and how to slaughter and care for meat. Under the tireless efforts of Father Junipero Serra, the mission herds rapidly expanded. They were Longhorns, descendants of the fighting bulls of Spain. Late-maturing and thin of flank, they had the speed of a racehorse. They were well equipped to harvest the California grass and cope with the environment of this wild and unsettled land. During this era, cow hides and tallow were the main articles of commerce, whereas meat had little value.

When John Marshall discovered gold in the sluice at John Sutter's mill in 1848, the "meat" of the cattle business boomed and the hide and tallow days came to an end. John Sutter had been a cattleman for some time, developing one of the largest herds in California. He should have grown rich from the new demand for meat, but the miners of '49, hungering for the yellow metal, slaughtered his cattle and laid waste to his holdings.

John Bidwell arrived in California in 1841, met John Sutter, and learned the cattle business from him. Bidwell took out Mexican citizenship to obtain a land grant of some 22,000 acres near Chico, California. He was methodical and conservative, did not overexpand his cattle herds, and practiced diversification. He built a mansion in 1869 at a cost of $56,000; it still stands on the campus of Chico State University, a symbol of one of the great California cat-

built of sagebrush. After boiling for several minutes, an egg shell was added to settle the grounds. It was strong enough to float a horseshoe. Since only strong men rode north, it took strong food and drink to cope with the elements.

Although Texas is considered the cattle land of the West, California was one of the first places to raise cattle as a business. Almost four centuries of history's aged and yellowed pages must be turned back if the cattle business of the Golden State is to be reviewed. Cattle followed closely on the heels of Cortés in his conquest of Mexico, and they accompanied the weary Spanish padres from mission to mission all the way up the coast along El Camino Real, the King's Highway.

California tales of grass and water, ranches and rancheros, the Spanish Don on his golden horse and silver outfit, the rodeos, fiestas, and señoritas portrayed a life known nowhere else. Under brilliant Cali-

tlemen. His great-grand-nephew, Floyd, carries on the tradition of raising top-performing Herefords on the ranch at Hat Creek, California.

Following the Gold Rush days, the transcontinental railroad was completed, bringing rapid settlement to California and all of the West. During this period, land grants were issued, and the Homestead Act became law, bringing barbed wire and windmills that rolled across the western horizon. Henry Miller, a butcher boy from Germany, arrived in San Francisco in 1850 with six dollars in his pocket. By 1916 he had acquired over a million acres of land and one million head of cattle—an unparalleled accomplishment. His business methods were copied by cattlemen throughout the West, and his brand became famous in California, Nevada, and Oregon.

Every hobo in the land was welcome for a handout at Miller's cattle camps, which were referred to as "the route of the dirty plate," since Miller did not want his cooks spending their time washing extra dishes. Feeding the hobos also meant that they would not make their own camp fires— cheap insurance against fire in his far reaching holdings.

In coping with "Old Man Drought," Miller had his foreman harvest, during wet years, wild oats and filaree as far up the draws and canyons as a team could pull a mower. This feed was stored, and during dry periods, he either sold hay to other cattlemen or bought their cattle for a song.

Miller had some hair-raising experiences, as when he was held up on the Pacheco Pass by Mexican bandits led by Chavez. They robbed him and then were

Oxbow Ranch
cattle drive, Prairie City, Oregon

going to kill him. He told the bandits that they were at liberty to kill his beef when they were hungry, but if they shot him they would have no beef. Miller was let go unharmed, but not before he asked "to borrow twenty dollars to pay my traveling expenses." The bandit leader gave him the money.

About two weeks later Miller was sitting in a bar in Gilroy, California, listening to the local gossip, when a good-looking Mexican walked in and ordered a drink. Miller recognized the voice, went over, and paid back the twenty dollars. "I always pay my bills."

California cattlemen were "riata" and "dally" hands, which meant they used a sixty- to seventy-foot rope to swing a big loop, and they rode a centerfire saddle. In contrast, the cowmen of the Southwest used a forty-foot rope tied hard and fast to the saddle horn on a double-cinch saddle. A California Indian cowboy was asked why he used such a big loop. "When I lasso 'em," he replied, "I lasso 'em all over." A big loop was apt to be more accurate.

When the War Between the States ended, the great days of the ranching industry began. As the men in gray came marching home, they found that the cattle numbers had greatly expanded, including mavericks—unbranded cattle, to be owned by whoever could rope them, then stamp them with a seal of ownership made by a hot iron brand. Texas had no money, but it had cattle. The Northeast had money but no cattle. The railroad had reached Kansas and Nebraska, so Texas had a ready cattle market. All they had to do was trail the animals to the railheads—two thousand miles north.

Texas, known as the Mother of Cattle Country, produced men like Charles Goodnight, who fought Indians and went broke twice before he put together a million-acre spread in the Texas Panhandle. Other cattle empires, like the Prairie Cattle Co. Ltd., owned 156,000 cows and controlled five million acres in 1883. In 1880 the XIT Ranch, comprised ten Texas counties covering over three million acres, used 200 miles of fencing, employed 150 cowboys, ran 1,000 horses and 150,000 head of cattle. Also in 1880 they put together another ranch in Montana as big as the Texas property. When trailing cattle between these two spreads, Mr. Doyce, the ramrodder, told his cowboys to keep their eyes on the North Star until they could wet their feet in the snowy waters of the Yellowstone.

Tom Moorhouse throws a "hoolihan" to catch horses for Moorhouse Ranch cowboys, Hall County, Texas.

Among the many great cattlemen were Francis Warren, John Chisum, Granville Stuart, and Teddy Roosevelt, who ranched in the harsh Badlands of the Dakotas. When Teddy left New York for the Dakotas, he was puny and frail, suffering from poor health. After a decade of ranching in the Badlands he came out strong, robust, and vigorous. He said, "The award belongs to the man in the arena whose face is covered with dirt, sweat and blood."

The biggest ranchers were usually the toughest and most resilient, like Richard King, owner of the giant King Ranch in southeast Texas. A riverboat merchant who plied the waters of the Rio Grande, King rode north from Brownsville, Texas, to Corpus Christi in 1852. He was amazed by the vast grasslands that stretched to the horizon, with thousands of wild horses roaming the land. He vowed that he would establish a cattle spread in that country and began by purchasing 15,500 acres for $300. Later he acquired another 53,000 acres for $1,800. Today the ranch is one of the largest in the world, with over 825,000 acres.

Robert Kleberg, a young attorney, married Richard King's daughter, Alice; when King died, Robert became ranch manager. He believed in science, so he hired trained animal breeders to develop outstanding cattle and horse studs through line, inbreeding, and crossbreeding. His efforts produced the Santa Gertrudis breed of cattle, $3/8$ Brahman and $5/8$ Shorthorn, which was widely adapted to western climatic and range conditions.

Captain King had many harrowing experiences, one of the most unusual having to do with a well-known outlaw. Soon after the end of the Civil War, a handsome young man riding a good-looking gray stallion stopped at the ranch for the night. The

next day the young drifter asked directions north, and at the time Mr. King admired the man's horse. A King Ranch cowboy led the young man down the road, pointing out the proper route. The young horseman traded mounts with the guide and told him to give his horse to Mr. King, compliments of Jessie James.

A thank you, Western style.

Men like King were too astute to think of ranching as an end in itself. Using their cattle profits, many invested in other businesses, like newspapers, banks, hotels, and stores. As their interests diversified, they gained political power. However, not all ranchers were land barons. In the early

Tom Moorhouse
enjoys his evening coffee in the "fly."
opposite

Bill Trampe
saddling up at dawn to work cattle
at the Lazy V. D. Land & Livestock
Ranch, Browns Park, Colorado

free-grass era, the trail ranchers rode across the Great Plains. They set up along immigrant routes and bought or were given worn-out cattle. In a few years they would own several hundred head and a homestead. Some of these homesteads are working ranches today. Though large spreads like the King Ranch of Kingsville, Texas, the Tejon Ranch of LeBeck, California, and the ZX Ranch of Paisley, Oregon, still exist, it is interesting to note that of the total number of beef cattle in the United States, most are in herds of one hundred or less.

Profits made in the cattle business following the Civil War attracted capital from England, with several large cattle syndicates being established from that country. One of the largest was the Swan Cattle Company, which owned 100,000 head of cattle managed by John Clay. The Wyoming spread was the size of the state of Connecticut, but the winter of 1886–87 wiped it out, and Clay went to work as a

"commission man" in the stockyards of Chicago.

Indeed, the drought of 1886–87 and the absence of Chinook winds broke the back of the cattle business, prompting a change in management from a year-round operation on open range to storing feed for winter feeding. As the story goes, just before Christmas, it rained, then a cold spell froze out all vegetation; snow fell to a two-foot depth, crusted over, and lasted until spring. It was called the "God of Winter" and the "Big Die Up."

Charles Russell, the cowboy artist, was living on the O.H. Ranch when Jesse Phelps, the manager, got a letter from the owner, Louie Kaufman, asking about the condition of his cattle. Russell painted a sketch, post-

Dan Russell,
Russell Ranches and Western
Rodeos, California and Nevada

Nig London
observes Quarter Horses at the R. A.
Brown Ranch, Throckmorton, Texas.

card size, and Phelps sent it to Kaufman. No letter was necessary. The painting illustrated an O.H. cow, skin and bones, standing humped up in snow surrounded by wolves. It was entitled "Waiting for a Chinook" and made Russell famous and rich.

Most cattlemen were top hands with horses. They did not ride the rough string, but were familiar with equine behavior and knew how to secure top performance from their mounts. They followed the horseman's code, feeding their horse before themselves. Many years ago I met Lee Vernon, a cattleman from Pittville, California. He was riding a splendid blazed-face sorrel horse. When I asked if the horse was any good, he replied: "By God, when you are on this horse, you are on horseback. He can do anything but count cattle." Ned Bognuda's daughter, Lil, of Little Valley, California, said her horse was "no damn good"; it did not like the smell of cows.

To answer the question of how a cattleman and a cowboy differ, Julius Trescony of San Lucas, California, has said, "A cowboy is a hired hand with guts and a horse, and a cowman is a businessman on horseback." In cattle circles, there is a saying: "Renowned and famous cowboys seldom become successful cowmen." But there are exceptions: Gene Rambo, cowboy cattleman of Shandon, California, was a native son of the Golden State, astute, modest, and soft-spoken. Gene spurred and dallied his way to four All Round World Cowboy championships in the International Rodeo Association while at the same time operating a ranch and building up one of the top cow-calf operations in the West, a feat that would be difficult to equal.

Gene followed the suicide circuit for a quarter of a century and competed in about nine hundred rodeos from as far north as

Double H

Calgary, Canada, to the southwest of the Lone Star State. The fierce will to win Gene displayed in the rodeo arena was also evident in the way he built up a high-producing cattle herd. Gene kept complete performance records on each cow in his herd. "Why guess," he says, "when you can measure performance with scales, microscope, and computer." Gene was also an expert in employing artificial insemination, using semen from the highest-performing bulls. Combining this sire selection with crossbreeding, he developed a profitable championship herd.

Branding cattle with a hot iron has been a custom in America since Cortés marked his herd with three Christian Crosses (+ + +), representing the Father, the Son, and the Holy Ghost. Today, as always, a brand is recognized above all other methods of proving ownership. Cattlemen are brand conscious. They think brands the year round. It is a common practice of cattlemen to whittle a brand out while sitting on a rail fence or doodling a brand while making a telephone call. They stamp brands on the cantle of their saddles, on the wings of their chaps and spur straps, their stationery, their checkbooks, and their auto hoods. Sons of cowmen have been known to carve their dad's brand on school desks.

To pick out a brand is serious and important business, as important as picking a name for a son. Sometimes the brand designates the cattle owner's name. Henry Miller, the early Cattle King of California, Nevada, and Oregon, had dreamed as a young boy in Germany of owning cattle with the Double H brand. Later, while sorting cattle hides in a slaughter house in San Francisco, he found a hide with that brand. A few years later he bought a herd of cattle in the San Joaquin Valley from the

Tom Moorhouse ropes a calf for branding on the Moorhouse Ranch, Hall County, Texas.

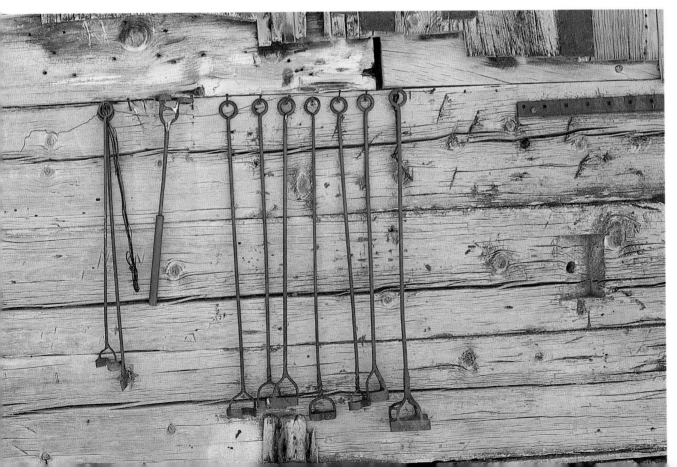

Branding irons hang on the side of a barn at La Vaca Co. ranch, Elko, Nevada.

Running W

Bar Double

The Frosty Acres snowman

Double Box Arrow

Cross Triangle

4 Bar M

Hildreth Brothers; the cattle carried the brand of his dreams. In the years that ensued, it was probably branded on more cattle than any other brand, except for the Running W of the King Ranch.

My father, W. J. Albaugh, traded a pair of corduroy pants for his Bar Double brand. My brother, Ed, has a ranch known as Frosty Acres, and his brand is a snowman's face, very well named.

Rustlers sometimes attempted to change the brands on stolen stock. This was usually done with a "running iron," a piece of iron about six inches long with a curved head. At times rustlers would attempt to doctor the registered iron by applying their hot iron over a wet sack to make the resulting brand look as if it had been applied months earlier. A notorious instance of changing a brand took place in southern Monterey County, California, when the famous Double H brand owned by Miller and Lux was changed to read Double Box Arrow. Another clever brand change was the Cross Triangle to the 4 Bar M.

Not all early cattlemen belonged to the saints' corral. Some mavericks fenced government land and claimed it as their own. They mistreated sheepmen, homesteaders, rustled cattle, and joined lynching parties. They drank their share of whiskey. Many years ago, after I addressed a cattlemen's meeting in Alturas, Modoc County, California, the chairman invited me to join him in a "shot in the heel" (a drink of whiskey). The bartender mixed my first drink and

quickly poured another, saying, "If you don't have a drink in both hands around here they will think you are a stranger."

Charles Russell said, "whiskey is a brave maker. It makes you do things you ordinarily would not do. If you like a man when you are sober, you can hardly keep from kissing him when you are drunk. If you don't like a man when you are sober, you don't want him in the same town when you are drunk."

Although cattlemen are extremely individualistic, they have from the early days banded together in organizations for the purpose of coping with problems such as rustlers, predatory animals, and detrimental legislation. Most states and many counties have cattlemen's associations affiliated with

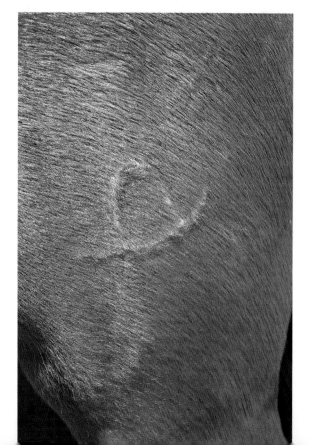

Branding
calves at the Moorhouse Ranch, Hall County, Texas

Sombrero
Ranch brand, Craig, Colorado

Wright
Dickinson saddling up at dawn to
work cattle, Lazy V. D. Land &
Livestock Ranch, Browns Park,
Colorado

the National Cattlemen's Association, head-quarted in Denver, Colorado. The cattlemen's wives have their own organizations, affiliated with American National Cattlewomen's Association.

Present-day cattlemen and women are well educated, having degrees from universities and colleges. They are well prepared to put scientific research and knowledge to work, utilizing computers, genetic engineering, and agricultural technologies to take some of the guesswork out of this old and colorful business. In the years ahead, it will be challenging for many producers to count on their cattle as their sole income. They will need to diversify, grow other crops, lease hunting and fishing rights, develop tourism with dude ranching and guiding pack trips. However, with their fierce individualism, strength of character, and dedication to their life-style, cattlemen will successfully meet the challenges of the future and continue to be our heroes of the saddle.

Linda Davis, rancher, C S Ranch, a Cimarron, New Mexico spread that has been operated 115 years by one family

RANCH FAMILY

TERESA JORDAN

A few weeks ago, I invited a friend over to sharpen knives. We had shared household chores before, using work as an excuse for conversation, but as we sat at the old oak table in my kitchen, talking to the rhythm of blade on stone, I realized how much I wanted him there that particular afternoon for that particular job. We did more than sharpen knives. We honed a ritual set deep in my bones.

I remember as a child long winter afternoons in the kitchen on our family's ranch in southeastern Wyoming, sitting at that same oak table while my father sharpened knives. Winters were the slack season, at least during the weeks between weaning and calving, and after the cattle were fed and assorted chores and catastrophes attended to, we had time for extended ritual. We had time for sharpening knives.

My brother and I would come home from school, and my father would set out the knives. He would gather up all he could find—the pocket knives that were as necessary an item of ranch attire as boots or socks or underwear; skinning knives; butcher knives; my mother's kitchen knives. He would cover the kitchen table with pages from *The Wall Street Journal* and arrange the knives in descending order according to size. He would set out his sharpening stone, the bottle of 3-in-1 Oil. My brother and I would sit down with cups of hot chocolate, my mother with a cup of coffee. And the sharpening would begin.

So would the stories. Once, when my

father was just out of school and riding a green-broke horse, he roped a wildcat. He was getting the colt used to a rope, touching the horse's legs, swinging the rope around its head, casting at twigs and sagebrush. He rode through some scrub pine and looked up to see a bobcat sitting in a tree. "Without thinking, I snapped the rope at the cat, just to scare him. Damned if I didn't catch him. Only lucky loop I ever had in my whole long life."

He would stop there, suddenly engrossed in the edge he honed on a blade.

"That cat," he would say in a few minutes, "was mad as seven hundred dollars, and it come right up the rope. Now, everyone knows that you don't tie hard and fast to the saddlehorn when you are riding a colt, but I'd done it anyway." He would stop again and inspect the edge of the knife. He would lick the hairs on the back of his hand, shave them clean with the newly razored edge. He would look up at us over the wire rims of his glasses. "The horse wasn't having any of it," he'd say, as he went back to sharpening. "He was bucking and kicking and squealing. And all the time that cat was trying to climb up the rope, just like he wanted to sit in the saddle with me. I was scared to fall off and scared to stick along for the ride."

And he would pick up another knife and hold it up to the light as if he could see the dullness there. Then he would breathe deeply, inhaling the scent of metal dust and oil-soaked newsprint, and set to sharpening just like it was the only thing on his mind. "So what *happened*, Dad," we would say, as we always said at this part of the story. He would work the knife slowly, as if trying to remember, as if thinking about something else entirely. Then, finally: "I cut the rope."

He'd gesture with the knife, cutting—with an almost audible pop—the rope held taut in our imaginations. "It was a brand-new rope, too," he'd add sadly, as the knife returned to the stone.

There were other stories. There was the one about the fat old cook who kept a six-gun in her apron pocket. One day someone on the hay crew complained about the grub. She stepped up behind him, took the pistol out of her pocket, and poked its cold steel barrel in the back of his neck. "Now you eat that," she said, pointing at his plate, "and tell me it's good." There was the story about the cowboy on a neighboring ranch who was caught in the '49 blizzard. He was a tough old coot, so his employer hauled food and supplies to everyone else first. When finally the boss chugged up to the camp in a D-8 Cat, the cowboy came barrelling out of his cabin. "It's about time you got here," he fumed. "I've been out of food for a week, and I'm *almost* out of whiskey." And then my father would tell about the time he drove a semi load of cattle to Montana and had a flat on an inside dual tire. While he worked to change it, the cows queued up in the truck above him and took turns pissing on his head. We *liked* that story.

We had stories of our own, of course. About the skunk who had taken up residence beneath the schoolhouse. About how Guy Vineyard had sassed Mr. Wade and ended up in the corner again. (We neglected to mention our roles in this particular drama.) And if our stories weren't as good, as colorful or funny or well-honed, as our father's, they were listened to with respect and attention. These were times of real conversation, of familial camaraderie. And I look back at them now and realize it's no wonder I don't like to sharpen knives alone.

For I am one of a small but identifiable breed. I am a ranch child. And that upbringing has marked me as distinctly, as indelibly, as pigment or nationality might. I no longer live on a ranch. Our family's ranch was sold a decade ago, a fate it shares with thousands of family ranches over the past fifteen years. I live in a city now. I work at a desk. But I carry with me the brand of my upbringing.

I am asked here to write about family on ranches, and I should begin with a few disclaimers. I loved growing up on a ranch, and except for a couple of years in high school, when I thought living fifty miles from town (and from my boyfriend) "totally uncool," I thrived there. In more recent years, I have traveled to ranch communities in a dozen western states, interviewing ranch women. I searched out women who

worked out of doors; their stories are inspiring. So I present here a positive picture. But the same factors that can make family life satisfying on a ranch—shared work, extended time together, and relative isolation from the outside world—can also make it difficult. Pastoral life can't escape the pathologies of human behavior any more than city life can, and the cost may be even higher far from town. An unkind man can hide the pickup keys from his wife, making isolation inescapable. A belittling wife can hack away at her husband's self-esteem more effectively when she works with him throughout the day. Children of battering parents may have less hope for outside intervention. Even insensitivity can wreak more havoc in isolation. As Dorothy Ross recalled in *Stranger to the Desert*, her memoir of turn-of-the-century ranch life in New Mexico, "It was a truly surprised and unhappy rancher who said: 'I can't figure out why my wife went crazy. Why, she ain't been out of the kitchen in twenty years!'" But many ranch families, much of the time, find their lives deeply satisfying.

Few occupations shape the whole family's life as much as ranching or farming does. They influence not only where the family lives, but, to greater or lesser degree, how all members of that family spend at least part of their time. Of course, there is tremendous diversity from ranch to ranch and from community to community. But on many family owned and operated ranches, everyone past infant stage participates to one degree or another.

I can't imagine defining a "typical" doctor's son or welder's daughter. But a fourteen-year-old ranch girl from Wyoming has at least a few things in common with a fourteen-year-old ranch boy from West Texas. They probably both know how to drive a stick shift and change a tire; they can feed and care for large animals, and if faced with an emergency when alone—say a cow has trouble giving birth—they can either solve the problem themselves or know where to go for help. They routinely make decisions that directly affect the family's income: Is that cow sick enough to doctor, or should they leave it alone and see how it's doing tomorrow? And they sometimes take on awesome responsibility. A neighbor of mine, Biddy Bonham, went into the cattle business at the age of sixteen with her sister. They each bought fifty heifers on money borrowed from their father and calved them out. Sometimes the responsibility is overwhelming. That same year, Biddy threw a rope at a sick calf and

missed him. Her father rode after the calf. When his horse tripped in a prairie dog hole, he was thrown and killed.

Ranch kids grow up knowing that the work they do is important, sometimes quite literally a matter of life and death. This gives them a particular adultness. And if they sometimes think their cousins from West Linn or L.A. are a bit, well, sissified, you can forgive them.

"Sometimes I think I ask them to be too grown up," says Linda Long about her daughters Cricket and Nondi—nine and six years old—in Nancy Kelly's documentary film *Cowgirls: Portraits of American Ranch Women.* "I'm sure that's a fault of mine.

Because you only have so much time to be a little girl, and you have all your life to be grown up and responsible."

"I hate getting yelled at the most," adds Nondi. "You're never in the right spot, you're always some place wrong, and it ends up being a longer day than you figured."

Ranch children as young as eight or nine often do their job alone. Although they start out with instructions, the nature of the work means that they frequently need to revise their plans. On a roundup, for instance, riders fan out over a pasture to gather the herd. A child may be asked to ride the far east ridge and push whatever cattle she finds toward the corral. With luck, everyone riding the pasture will arrive with their cattle at the corral at the same time. But she rides the east ridge and doesn't see anything. She wonders if she should leave the ridge and try and help someone else, or should she stick with the original plan. Or she finds a hole in the fence and sees fifty pair in the neighbor's pasture. If she rides after them, she will get to the corral later than everyone else. If she doesn't, someone will have to come back for them later. Many young ranch kids I know talk about these moments of uncertainty with dread. But they make some sort of decision, and they act on it. If they live in a supportive family where the fact that they made a decision is applauded even when the outcome isn't perfect, they grow into decisive and confident adults.

Children who grow up in agriculture have a chance, from an early age, to learn skills and gain recognition for them. Ranch work requires such aptitudes as horse training, sheep shearing, roping, and harness repair, not to mention knowledge of veterinary medicine, auto mechanics, plumbing, electricity, irrigation, carpentry, and

DeeDee
Dickinson working on a corral at
the family's Rife Ranch in
southwestern Wyoming

Jean
Dickinson building a corral
at the Rife Ranch

bookkeeping. As a child gravitates toward those areas that interest him and masters them, he earns that most coveted of designations—he makes a good hand. Organizations like High School Rodeo, 4-H, and Future Farmers of America add further reward for these skills, which are not only personally satisfying but intimately involved with the family's welfare.

All this sounds like a lot of responsibility from a young age, and it is. But with that responsibility comes an independence, a freedom and mobility. From the time I was six or seven, I could saddle my own horse and ride where I pleased. I might ride seven miles up the road to visit the postmaster, or nine miles over the bluffs to see my Aunt Marie. Or I might just go to my secret place, a little grotto on Chugwater Creek I was sure no one else had ever discovered. I spent a lot of time there, making whistles out of the broad-bladed grass and telling my old bay, Buddy, how sad I was or how happy, what I would be

when I grew up, or how I'd never leave him.

For kids who like animals, a childhood on a ranch is an extraordinary gift. But children who don't take to critters or work outdoors may have a rougher time. Generally, girls fare better. If they don't want to work outside, they can follow more domestic pursuits. But a boy who would rather read or play the piano than punch cows may feel pressure. My brother didn't like horses much and would rather have hidden away with a stack of books than engage in almost any sort of ranch work. My parents tried to understand and support him, but he still felt pressure from them and from the community at large to be a good rider, a good roper, a good hand. He learned these things, but he never enjoyed them. I suspect, were he to write his own memoir of growing up a ranch kid, it would be different from my own.

If the cattle industry offers no greater guarantee of golden childhood than city life, it at least has the potential to provide fundamentally different familial relationships. A ranch provides an almost preindustrial structure to family. Home and the workplace are one and the same. Not all rural families work together: some wives work in town; some husbands work for wages at a nearby coal mine or neighboring ranch while their wives take care of the home place; some kids, for a variety of reasons, don't participate at all. But when the ranch is a shared endeavor, real partnership is possible.

Most ranch kids, for instance, spend more time with their fathers than do their counterparts in town, and they understand the family work more completely. "Our kids understand our business," Montana ranch woman Linen Bliss once told me. "Eleven-year-old Scott knows exactly what we do because he does it, too." Linen grew up differently. Her father was a stockbroker. Her mother used to say that the brokerage was a gamble, so when the fourth-grade teacher asked Linen what her father did, she said he was a gambler.

Had my own father's work been different, I doubt my brother and I would have had the chance to know him well. He is a serious man, not much given to play or drawn to children. He is also deaf, so children's chatter perplexes him. But if he didn't know how to play with us, he knew how to teach, and in the long hours we spent riding horseback together or sitting in the cab of a pickup, he passed on what he knew. He taught us how to put a rein on a colt by shifting our weight in the saddle, how to tie a hackamore knot and throw a hoolihan, how to talk to an unbroke horse or approach a mad bull, how to double-clutch the stock truck, how to read the horizon, how to drink, how to negotiate a deal. And if he came in after a hard day tired and grumpy, dragging his footprints out with the seat of his pants, we understood because we followed behind him and felt the same fatigue.

The ranch also gave us the chance to know a side of our mother we might have missed had we lived in town. Although she didn't work outside, she was central to the operation of the ranch. She was a wife and mother, but she was also a business partner: she handled the books and paperwork and kept the ranch stocked with equipment and

Little ranchers at the Texas Ranch Roundup, Wichita Falls, Texas
top

Peggy Brown, grandmother, with her daughter, Betsy Bellah, and grandson, Brad—three generations on the R. A. Brown Ranch, Throckmorton, Texas

A young cowboy practicing roping before an attentive audience at the National Ranching Heritage Center, Museum of Texas Tech University, Lubbock, Texas

4-H exhibit of
beef cattle at the Island County Fair,
Washington

other supplies. Kids often take for granted the extraordinary labor of housekeeping, cooking, and rearing a family; it was harder to overlook our mother's daily contribution to the running of the ranch. When she dragged in at the end of the day after visiting implement dealers in three distant towns, delivering half a dozen damaged tractor tires, shopping groceries to feed the hay crew, and picking up an irrigator at the employment agency who just happened to be both drunk and fresh, we took the cue from our father to pitch in and unload the car or fix dinner. He stressed that the ranch was a team effort, that one person's work was as important as another's.

"On a ranch," said Linen Bliss, "you learn to respect each other for what you can do. Sometimes you lose patience with your loved ones before you would an outsider, but you learn to recognize each other's limits and strengths and work around those." Linen felt shared work brought the family together. "A lot of families are only together for recreation," she explained, "and sometimes it's hard to have fun playing together. I look at people stuffed in station wagons, a thousand miles from home, broken down with a flat tire. The kids are hot and their popsicles are melting all over the back seat. I wonder how that could possibly be fun."

"We've had so many happy times out there with the kids and without television," added Linen's neighbor, Martha Gibbs. "We can communicate with them, work with them, play cards with them. Sometimes during the school year, when we live in town, it's hard to sit down and have a

our marriage is traditional in any respect."

My mother experienced a similar content. When I was in college, I once asked her if she hadn't missed having a career of her own. I had brought home books by Gloria Steinem and Betty Friedan, but she had no interest in them. "You can't imagine," she told me as we sat at the kitchen table talking late into the night, "how satisfying this work has been." She gestured then, the sweep of her hand taking in the kitchen, the house, my father sleeping upstairs, the conversation. Everyone is off and about, involved in other things."

If working together lets children know their parents better, it also lets the parents know each other. "Everything Ike and I have done, we've done together," Wyoming rancher Gwynne Fordyce told me, and "I feel I've contributed to what we've accomplished. I've done more than just run the home. When I cook for help or work cows, I know I've contributed to the support and income of the ranch."

Ike agreed. "I think 80 percent of all the cattle work we've done in twenty years, we've done ourselves. We simply wouldn't have done as well if Gwynne didn't work."

Gwynne came to ranching from an eastern background, and rural life gave her a way to combine marriage with career. "I feel that being a ranch wife and mother is much more demanding of me as an individual than a career would have been. I think that I would have felt unfulfilled had I not married and had children and been a part of my husband's business. It would be very difficult for me to live with someone who went to work at nine and came home at five and never discussed his concerns. Ike and I have the same goals. I don't feel

whole of that ranch, which had occupied her for a quarter of a century fifty miles from town. I finally began to understand what she and my father had been telling me all along. My mother, the ranch wife, *had* her own career.

The job of ranch wife is different for everyone who fills it. For women in an unhappy marriage or those who simply don't like living in the country, it can be a torment; for others, it provides deep satisfaction. "I can put in one hell of a day on the ranch," said Martha Gibbs, "throw a circle [ride a long distance after cattle] that would kill somebody in town. Or I can get up at dawn, work really hard all morning branding, and then come in and have dinner ready for thirty people in half an hour because I've prepared it all the night before. During calving, I'm covered with crud from head to toe, with blood all over my hands. And I love it. I love any day when we can all go out and ride and work together and drag in exhausted at night. I can't describe what the ranch means to me—it's intangible. But I have a feeling of gathering myself together and having time to think, to appreciate what life is all about."

I'm thankful for my ranch background, and perhaps I hark back to it too fondly. But if I plead guilty to a strain of romance, so do many ranch folk I know. "There's nothing greater than a family in the country," says Wyoming rancher Nicki Taylor unabashedly. "Oh, it's great out here," says another ranch mom I know. "It's just like they say—the family that hays together stays together." Another injects a more realistic note. "Sometimes," she says, "it seems like too much togetherness and not enough money. But no, I wouldn't trade it for the world."

Lisa Shurtz,
rancher and cattle buyer, feeds cattle
on the La Vaca Co. spread,
Elko, Nevada
top

Maggie Bentz
at the Sombrero Ranch, Browns
Park, Colorado

THE BUSINESS OF RANCHING

ELMER KELTON

Like many another ranchman of his time, my grandfather used to carry his ranch records in his shirt pocket, penciled into a small tally book, which bore the imprint of a livestock commission house on the Fort Worth Stockyards. That little book held everything he felt inclined to commit to paper: the number of cattle he had turned into or removed from each pasture, how many calves he branded, how many he weaned, their sales and shipping weights. He might note the feed he bought, the times and amounts he fed, the day he releathered a certain windmill.

For a small cowman still following the traditions of the horse-and-wagon days, operating in a time when the federal income tax system remained relatively simple and benign, this was bookkeeping enough.

Profit and loss were easy to figure. You started the year with a certain amount of money in the bank. If you had more when the year ended, you had made a profit. If you had less, the year showed a loss. Understanding that principle did not require a high-school education.

The trouble was, for too many ranchmen too many years showed a loss, often in a long and unbroken sequence. They did so in the classic days of the open range. They still do.

My father was a working cowboy and a ranchman all his life. He was also a good storyteller in the old oral tradition. As a boy I liked to hang my legs off the bunkhouse porch on a cool summer's evening, listening to him and the cowboys swap

Jody Bellah and Joe Self checking the sale order of bulls for the R. A. Brown Ranch bull sale, Throckmorton, Texas

yarns. He would tell about ranches on which he had punched cattle in his youth throughout the Midland and Odessa country of West Texas. Usually the stories were humorous, but all too often they had a dark ending. This outfit went broke in the slump of 1922, or that one in 1925. This ranchman turned everything over to the receivers in 1929, that one in 1932.

There was not much glamour or romance in Dad's stories of ranching, certainly not when it came to the economic side. He had grown up listening to the wolf scratch at the back door, and he remained wary of that wolf all his life. He did not have to rely on others' experiences to know how precarious ranching could be. While still a young man working for cowboy wages, he bought a little string of cows with borrowed money in 1928.

When the crash came a year later, the lender stayed with him. If thrown upon a disastrously overcrowded market, those cows would not have begun to repay what he owed on them. Dad kept his cattle through the long Depression years, pasturing them on leased land and tending them in whatever spare time he could find or make, feeding them out of the wages he earned as a foreman on the McElroy Ranch in Upton and Crane counties of West Texas. Not until the eve of World War II did he finally pay them off free and clear.

He was well acquainted with the wolf.

When controls came off of cattle prices after the war, it looked as if Dad might finally enjoy a modicum of prosperity. But in 1947 his lease expired on the ranch he had been using for most of the decade. The landowner's sons had returned from the war and, very understandably, wanted to begin ranching. Dad found no other suitable lease land near enough to his job, so with a reluctance that bordered on grief, he sold his cattle.

It was one of the luckiest things that ever happened to him; for out of the hot and dry west came another of the ranchman's most unforgiving enemies, more deadly even than a Depression market: drought.

Almost from the day the final truck hauled the last of his Half H cattle away from the shaky old loading chute, that ranch began falling into the longest, meanest, most blistering drought in the memory of anyone then living. For ten years the place

Working cattle into pens for shipping, Mee Ranch, King City, California

he had vacated in the Crane County sand-hills never saw enough rain at one time to head out a half-decent crop of grass.

The landowner's sons learned a bitter lesson in ranch economics, and all of them turned to other professions.

It is an axiom that ranching, like agriculture in general, is a good life but often a poor living.

Today, with the many unavoidable expenses involved, close attention to the business aspects of ranching is more vital than ever, because costs are high and margins are thin or non-existent. My grand-father's tally book is no longer anywhere near enough.

It would be a gross oversimplification to infer that good bookkeeping began with the contemporary generation of ranchmen. Ranching was always a business. The operator who did not regard it as one was unlikely to remain in business very long, especially if he ranched on any scale. The

bigger the ranch, the bigger and more numerous the wolves prowling around the back door. Many of the pioneer ranchmen gravitated into that trade from a background in other businesses. Richard King of South Texas, for example, had been a ship's captain and was accustomed to keeping detailed ledgers and accounts. When, in 1854, he bought the first tract of what was to become the famous King Ranch, he built on that experience to put together the largest ranch in Texas.

The King Ranch evokes a highly romantic image, but behind the image is a carefully operated business run by people who know where they have been and where they intend to be tomorrow. Out front, in the advertising and in occasional media coverage, you see cowboys and horses and fine red cattle. What you don't often see—though it is very much a part of the operation—is an efficiently run office where the books are kept. And the bookkeeping has been computerized for a decade or more.

A wealth of rangeland folklore has come out of the old Matador Ranch in the Texas Panhandle. Those stories are varia-

tions on all the classic tales about cowboy life. The ranch's name has even become a verb. When ranch hands in that region speak of "matadoring" cattle, they mean handling them fast and rough in the wildest cowboy tradition.

But behind that image as well is the reality of a businesslike operation. The Matador was founded in 1883 by Scottish investors attracted by exaggerated stories of the beef bonanza. But with the canny foresight for which the Scots are famous, they built slowly and solidly, always with one eye on the cattle and the other on the books.

The old Matador headquarters office building is preserved intact today on the grounds of the Ranching Heritage Center in Lubbock, Texas. I once heard a former Matador cowboy declare it to have been the most important single element of the ranch. For him, that was because he went there each month to draw his paycheck. But from a broader perspective, it was the heart that pumped blood to the ranch's most distant extremities.

Like my grandfather, my father kept records in a shirt-pocket tally book. I still treasure a number of them. But Dad was foreman for a large ranching company, and the rough notes from his tally books passed into large permanent ledgers in the ranch office, overseen by an old Norwegian bachelor bookkeeper who knew little about cattle and less about horses but had a keen sense of the bottom line.

He always wore a clean white shirt and was paid far better than any of the cowboys. He lived in a house assigned to him alone, while the hands shared a bunkhouse. They never questioned the rightness of this arrangement. A mistake on their part might at worst have lost a few cattle

or crippled a horse. A mistake on *his* part could have crippled the company. It never happened, of course. Tom Schreiner knew the ranch was a business, and it was his job to see that it operated as one.

While failure to keep careful records makes it very difficult for a ranching operation to remain viable, it does not necessarily hold that having a good set of records is a guarantee of success. It may only mean that the ship sinks in the daylight rather than in the darkness.

A case in point is one of the most impressive ranch bookkeeping systems I ever saw, used by a large, diversified operation on the Texas rolling plains. The records were intricate. Every cowboy, every farmhand made a full accounting of each day's activities. He tallied how many hours he had spent working at one task, how many at another. If he drove a pickup, he entered the daily mileage and even divided that mileage into the amount spent on the cow-calf operation, or the stocker cattle grazing wheat pasture, or maintenance work on fences and windmills. Each individual segment of the ranch's several enterprises became a separate "profit center" in the best manner of a major industrial corporation. The hours of each man's labor, the miles driven in each vehicle, were carefully apportioned. At any given time the manager could tell just how much each enterprise was costing and whether it was truly a profit center or, God forbid, a loss center.

Unfortunately, the loss centers prevailed. The cattle-market crash of 1973 and the farming depression that began soon afterward slowly dragged the whole operation under. The best-kept set of books I ever saw did not prevent the ranch from going into bankruptcy. But they documented the process beautifully.

There is no question that the costs of ranching are far higher today than ever before in terms of the prices paid for cattle, sheep, and other livestock commodities. Forty years ago an oldtime Texas sheepman proudly told me about the years he had spent in his youth, sleeping in a sheep-camp tent and sometimes sleeping out with no tent at all. He lived on coffee and bacon, beans, bread, and mutton, spending virtually nothing while he built his flock into a prosperous enterprise.

"I lived like a coyote," he declared, "but in those days we could still do it."

Even at the time he spoke, such a life was no longer possible, or at least no longer practical. In his youth the pasturage was often free for the taking, especially for a man drifting his sheep across the open country. At worst, it might cost him a few cents per head per year. If he lived like a coyote, as he described it, any helpers he might have to hire would live no better and extract relatively little money from his pocket. Wages were notoriously poor. In the main, they still are.

Even at the time of the long 1950s drought, which afflicted the Southwest for the better part of that decade, a cattleman could haul ten calves to the auction sale in town and use the check to buy a good new pickup. Not long ago a ranchman using a stub pencil and a yellow pad showed me that he would have to sell more than thirty calves now to buy a pickup of similar value.

Even using the best of modern herd and range management, it is unlikely that he can raise many more calves on a given acreage than he could have done thirty-odd years ago. So, in effect, buying a new pickup today requires the production from three times the acreage than it used to.

You'll see a lot of battered, brush-

years have been so few and far between since the cattle crash of 1973 that major capital expenditures, not to mention a lot of routine maintenance, have been deferred in hope of better times.

This crunch has forced many ranchmen to seek new and sometimes exotic ways to augment livestock income. For many, especially small operators who could spare the time, this has meant taking outside work and relegating the ranch chores to evenings and weekends. Or, if this was not practical, getting the wife a job in town.

Dude ranches began several generations ago in many areas of the West, particularly the more scenic desert and mountain regions, in response to other visitations by the same wolf that haunted my father and grandfather. Wrangling tourists was often more profitable than herding sheep or cattle. These guest ranches remain a fixture across the West, as often as not in combination with the bonafide livestock operation that periodically needs to be subsidized through the lean times by a transfusion of city-dweller dollars.

New variations have developed, particularly in private-ownership states such as Texas, where the ranchman does not require the blessing of a small army of federal-land employees for every move he makes. Dude ranches are scarce in Texas, except in a few specific scenic areas, but hunting has become an important—even vital—income source for a significant percentage of that state's ranching industry. No one will ever know how many ranch operators have been rescued from a session in bankruptcy court by Houston and Dallas hunters willing to pay to invade their white-tail-deer herd.

Some wildlife specialists declare that the hill country of southwest Texas has more whitetail deer and wild turkeys today

scarred old pickups on ranches these days. As a good cowboy has said, it takes a lot of baling wire to hold a ranch together.

It takes a great deal more as well. It takes a close watch on expenditures, because they have a dismaying tendency to exceed livestock income. An Oklahoma ranchman not long ago made a thirty-minute talk about survival, then summed it all up in one sentence: "Never buy a new nail if you can straighten out an old one."

Travel over the ranch country today and you'll see a lot of windmills, a lot of fences badly in need of major repair, if not replacement. Visit ranch headquarters, and you may see old buildings crying for a visit by a good crew of carpenters. Profitable

than even the Indians ever saw. For fifty years or more, ranch owners have consciously worked to build up the native wild game as a self-renewing natural resource. Night-grazing deer in the highway rights-of-way have become a traffic hazard far beyond the hill country. They thrive in areas where they had not been seen since pioneer times, because landowners have done whatever was necessary to bring these animals back.

A basic limitation on native wild game as a source of income is the seasonality of the harvest. Most hunting is concentrated in a six- or seven-week period in the fall. To extend hunting income for year-round cash flow, many ranches have introduced exotic game from other parts of the world.

This is especially prevalent in the Texas hill country because the habitat is friendly to a wide variety of exotic deer, antelope, and other species. Legally, these animals are regarded as livestock rather than wild game, and limited hunting seasons do not apply.

Probably no better example can be found than the YO Ranch near Kerrville, Texas. Established more than a century ago by pioneer ranchman, merchant, and Texas Ranger Charles Schreiner, the ranch continues to be operated by his descendants. It still has one of the Southwest's most famous herds of Longhorn cattle, much like those the founder used to send up the trail to Kansas railroads more than a hundred years ago. But it also has a variety of exotic

Y O Ranch
Longhorn cows

Zebra at
the Y O Ranch, Kerrville, Texas

animals from widely scattered parts of the world, some for hunting, some just for looking at. A major part of the ranch income is derived from hunters seeking trophies and from safari groups that just seek the thrill of viewing and perhaps photographing wild animals in the open—a sight they might otherwise have to travel to Africa for. For these visitors the ranch provides hunting lodges and even a rustic mess hall, which still feeds a crew of working cowboys.

Old Captain Schreiner would be surprised if he could see what has happened to his ranch. But because he was first and last a businessman, he would understand the necessity for improvising to survive in changing times.

Oil and gas income has been the sal-

Hereford bull show at the National Western Stock Show, Denver, Colorado

vation of many ranchmen in the Southwest—and, now and then, the ruination of their offspring. But having it is usually just the luck of the draw, as rodeo cowboys would say. The minerals are either there or they are not, and the landowner's input usually is little more than deciding whether to accept a driller's lease contract or to hold out for more favorable terms. Only a small minority have ever developed their own wells. A few who have done so, however, have become fabulously wealthy, enough so that they were able to continue ranching and perhaps even expand.

An old cow-country joke tells about a ranchman who is asked what he would do if he suddenly came into a million dollars of oil money. He studies a moment, then replies, "I would just keep on ranching until I used it up."

There seems to be a myth about the ranching industry, that rapid changes are a relatively new thing and that ranching in the past enjoyed a long spell of stability, or "normalcy," that oldtimers now regard as "the good old days." In truth, ranching never stood still. From the time it began to take the general form that we know today, starting basically in Texas and initially following traditional patterns established in Mexico, it has undergone constant change.

Early cattle raisers had to find their markets near to home, a limitation on herd sizes because there was a local demand for only so much beef and no more. The gradual westward extension of railroads and growth of slaughtering plants in the Midwest were the impetus for the first great post-Civil War trail drives north from Texas, patterned after pre-war drives that had taken cattle to Missouri, Illinois, and even New York. Trail driving itself was a major innovation, opening new horizons for cattlemen. But after only a relatively few years it was made obsolete by the building of railroads into the producing areas of the West.

Great terminal livestock markets soon grew up at major concentration points along these railroads, usually in conjunction with huge packing plants. For a couple of generations of ranchmen, big markets like Chicago, Omaha, Denver, and Fort Worth became the major sales outlets from the Canadian border to the Rio Grande.

This system lasted longer than the trail drives, but it began a long decline as better highways and larger trucks reduced dependence upon rails. Beginning in the 1930s and catching fire after World War II, local livestock auctions siphoned away an ever-increasing percentage of the central terminals' trade, gradually bleeding them to death.

L & M Feedlots
overlooking the Columbia River,
Pasco, Washington

Semi rig
ready to load sale cattle at the
Cottonwood Ranch, O'Neill Basin,
Nevada

Most today are shadows of their former selves. The big central packing plants became obsolete and were replaced by smaller but more modern and efficient facilities strategically located in areas where the livestock are raised and fed. The great Chicago stockyards were closed several years ago. Most of the Fort Worth stockyards were torn down to make room for retail businesses. The old stockyards hotel has been remodeled into a rustic tourist center. North Fort Worth's biggest attraction for a time became Billy Bob's Texas, one of the most famous country-western night spots in the nation, built on the same ground where ranchmen, commission men, and buyers whittled, spat, and dickered over millions of cattle.

Today the electronic age has a foot firmly wedged in the door of livestock marketing. Cattle and sheep are being sold over computer networks and by video. Several variations on these methods have been tried, each with its successes and its failures.

Simplest is a telephone conference call, in which animals are auctioned off in a generally conventional manner except that buyers and sellers are but voices to one another, and the livestock are seen only through the eyes of a grader, who describes each lot before it is sold.

Next is a computer network that lists livestock for sale with full physical descriptions, available to any prospective buyer who has access to the proper computer

Simplot Land & Livestock feedlot, Grandview, Idaho

Piles of processed feed at the Simplot Land & Livestock feedlot, Grandview, Idaho

terminal. At an appointed time the sale begins. Buyers are connected to the central computer through a telephone modem system. The sale progresses lot by lot on computer printout rather than by voice. When bids are called for, a buyer can punch in his identification code and his bid. After a specified period has elapsed—perhaps fifteen or twenty seconds—without a bid's being raised, the coordinator declares the animals sold or all bids rejected. Each participant keeps up with the action through his own printout.

Video is the newest marketing tool. Still in its infancy, video has already sold hundreds of thousands of cattle and a significant number of sheep. A sale agency sends a camera team and a qualified grader to visit each livestock consignment on its home ranch or fields. The animals are videotaped and the tape edited into segments usually running about two to three minutes per lot. A voice-over announcer

describes the terms under which the animals will be delivered, their expected weights, and so on. The earliest video sales were conducted like conventional auctions, except that the cattle or sheep were not physically in the ring. Auctioneer, buyers, and spectators looked at them on television monitors via videotape.

The most recent innovation is to telecast these sales by satellite. Anyone who has access to a satellite-receiving dish anywhere in the continental United States can watch and submit bids by telephone. Prospective buyers preregister so their credit can be confirmed, a normal procedure for new buyers even in most conventional auctions. They are given an opportunity to preview the livestock by a dry-run transmission of the tapes just prior to the sale. They can telephone auction headquarters by long distance and take part in the live bidding as they watch the animals offered lot by lot on a television set in their home,

Spotters
doing their work during the R. A.
Brown Ranch bull sale

office, feedlot, even their barn. While the most prevalent methods of selling livestock remain local or regional auctions and direct trade between buyer and seller, the electronic age has arrived.

In an effort to survive long depressions in the cattle business, many western cattlemen long ago swallowed their pride and added sheep to their operations. Historically, sheep have tended to show a better return on investment than cattle. I remember my father's amusement, long ago, when a neighbor who had turned to the woolies advised him to do the same. "Buck," he declared, "they're mortgage-liftin' *thangs.*"

Dad chuckled over that for a long time. But there came a point in his life when he *did* try sheep. He found his neighbor was right.

Ranchmen have tried to meet the recent economic crises by changing the type of cattle they raise. Thirty years ago it was no challenge to look at a herd and identify the breed. Across most of the West there were basically just two: the reddish, bald-faced Hereford and the coal-black Angus. In the Southwest the Brahman influence was also prominent, even dominant in hot southern climates.

The floodgates of immigration flew open in the 1960s and 1970s. One exotic breed after another was introduced from various parts of the world, as producers tried to figure out what the beef market really wanted. Crossbreeding, long distrusted by the mainstream cattleman, became the norm instead of the exception. Today it is rare to find a calf the same color as the cow it follows.

Grazing systems have undergone rigorous experimentation in an effort not only to produce more beef and mutton but to preserve and improve the range. The Sonora Experiment Station in Texas pioneered a number of rotation grazing methods, probably the most popular of these a four-pasture rotation system that bears the name of its originator, Dr. Leo Merrill. In this system, four pastures of similar carrying capacity are grouped, three of them bearing the full grazing load while the fourth rests for four months. The full cycle requires sixteen months, so that the rest period for each pasture is in a different season than the one before.

A much more revolutionary and controversial method, which has gripped the attention of ranchmen all over the West, is the Savory method, introduced in this country toward the end of the 1970s by Rhodesian conservationists Allan Savory and Stan Parsons. Their program is complex, but at the heart of it is the division of large pastures into small portions known as paddocks, usually from eight to perhaps as many as sixteen in a group. The entire herd is grazed on one paddock at a time while all the others rest. Rotation may be as frequent as every two or three days. Conventionally, these paddocks are built in a wagonwheel or pie-shape configuration, with one common watering place in the center.

Sale ring inside the barn, R. A. Brown Ranch bull sale

Double J. A.
Land & Livestock herd of
commercial cows are lined up for
the second day of a four-day cattle
drive covering sixty miles.

When it is time to move the animals, a gate at the central waterlot is thrown open to the fresh pasture. After a little acclimation, most animals readily move to the next pasture on their own. In fact, it can be downright dangerous to stand in their way when the gate is opened, so eager are they to get at the fresh grazing.

This method has its strong proponents, who claim it results in more even grazing of all vegetation, increases total production, and improves the range. It also has its critics and doubters, who argue that the heavy stocking, even for a short period, has to be detrimental to the range in the long run. In any case, it is far removed from the traditional practice of turning animals loose on the open range to rustle for themselves. My father probably never would have tried it. One of my brothers, however, has.

The Savory method requires close supervision, for its intensified nature means that a problem considered minor under normal circumstances becomes major almost immediately, especially any breakdown in the watering system. The other side of the coin is that all the animals are in one group, easily seen and tended. This method, despite its complexities, usually requires less labor.

The jury is still out on its long-term environmental effect. Many ranchmen have claimed rapid improvement of their grass. Others have been so discouraged that they have torn down their paddock fences and reverted to traditional pastures. In the long run, success or failure of the Savory method probably will depend upon the management of each individual ranch. And that would appear to sum up the future of the ranching industry as a whole. It is a way of life, to be sure. But to survive, it must also remain a business.

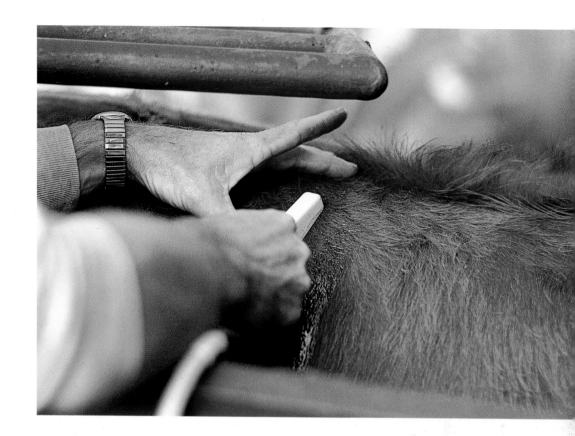

Measuring the percentage of fat at the Beef Cattle Evaluation Center, Cal Poly State University, San Luis Obispo, California

~~~~~~

CLOCKWORK AGRICULTURE

WILLIAM KITTREDGE

~~~~~~

There is a famous scene in the film *Rancho Deluxe*, set over around Livingston and written by Tom McGuane, a knowledgeable Easterner transplanted to the ranchland culture of Montana, in which an experienced man complains about pickup trucks. "Everybody I know," he says, "has ruined their life over the price of a new pickup truck."

Or something like that. It's a scene people in Montana remember, likely because it smacks of devastating truth. Everybody has his own version of that line, probably because everybody connected with agriculture has lived his own version of the wreck.

One of my earliest memories with any continuity comes from the summer I was five years old, 1937, in the heart of the Great Depression. My parents were moving from a rented house in Klamath Falls to the MC Ranch, huge properties my grandfather had got hold of in Warner Valley, over east on the high, landlocked fringes of the Great Basin. My mother had come to marriage with a lot of fine hardwood furniture, enough to make up a truckload, and that furniture was loaded on a ranch truck, and it was being driven to the ranch in Warner by an employee and drinking crony of my father's, a man named Jack Ray.

It seemed to a five-year-old boy like we drove all day and then we came to our wreck. It was beyond the lumber-milling town of Bly that the farm truck overturned down in the juniper trees, so far from the

Standard-size hay bales

~~~~

highway we almost didn't notice. Jack Ray, it seemed, had been *at the whiskey*, and my mother's furniture, including her great black grand piano, was mostly a collection of splintered hardwood.

Served her fair enough, some people thought, like my grandmother on my father's side, who considered hauling a piano out to the ranch an act of overweening arrogance. I like to imagine the sounds of those piano wires snapping and twanging as the wreck settled, with Jack Ray rubbing his head and feeling around for his pint. Because Jack Ray wasn't hurt. My father said Jack would die in bed, and he did.

That wreck cast a considerable shadow. My grandfather had strict rules, one of which was *never hire the people you drink with*. Through loyalty to old friends, my father had made a philosophic mistake. Implications reverberated all down the line. To this day, my mother hates Jack Ray. When I reminded her of Jack recently, she almost spat. "That damned fool," she said.

My mother eventually got another piano, and she never lost her belief that art and music could survive in the rancher world she had come to when she married my father. But that wreck seemed to prove that my grandfather was correct in his bottom-line way of understanding the world, and that my mother and her piano and all it stood for were mostly pointless and a pain in the neck. The redress never came, not in this life.

An ancient world was changing, and my people were on the leading edge of the conversion. And they knew it; they gloried in it. They were vital, somewhat heedless, and the idea that they were connected to great doings in the world inhabited them and drove them every moment.

Warner Valley, where we moved that spring of 1936, when I was four years old and prime in my readiness to witness paradise, was in what I think of as its prelapsarian stage, a great landlocked oasis valley lost out in an endlessness of high sagebrush deserts along the Oregon/Nevada border, the property fenced, tamed—but not too much. It was clear we had stumbled onto one of the last great innocent and untouched places, and that ours was rare good luck.

The last thirty-six miles of washboard gravel county road twisted over the Warner Mountains to end with us. Beyond, to the east, wagon roads twisted in among the rimrocks and alkaline flats to an endlessness of high desert; but, essentially, the way in to our valley was the way out. There was no electricity except that generated for house lights by the Delco power plant with its rows of glass battery cells. There was no functioning telephone at all, although there had been some time in the past; up in the Adel Store there was an old hand-crank instrument on the wall, and there was telephone wire hanging loose from a line of spindly poles along the road to town.

In February and early March the creeks draining out of the Warner Mountains to the west, Deep Creek and Twenty Mile, would flood and fill the vast tule beds until at sunset the swamps on the far east side of the valley shimmered with water, like a lake. The unbroken peat soil under those miles of swamp was eight feet deep in places. In spring and fall the water birds, the cinnamon teal and red heads and canvasback and mallards, and the blue-winged teal and the green-winged teal and the varieties of white geese and the lesser Canadians and the Canada geese would come migrating through in undulating vee-

Open-range grazing, with the Cottonwood Ranch hay meadow in the background, O'Neill Basin, Nevada

shaped rafts beyond numbering. Buffle-heads and avocet, and California quail in the brush, along with ring-necked pheasants introduced from Manchuria.

The point here is abundance, and great hunting, an overwhelming property thronging with natural life, and what my family did with it. My grandfather had come up from poverty, making his way on borrowed money, and he was a true desert cattle rancher, which means he had come to what he owned through years devoted to a hard horseback notion of life. He was mainly interested in his cattle and how they were doing, beef on the hoof, for sale.

For my grandfather, in that beginning, Warner must have been simply the ultimate answer to a lifetime of yearning, thousands of acres of meadow on the high side of the valley, cut with sloughs and willows for shelter, where he could winter his stock on native hay stacked with the beaver slides. The MC was a grant ranch. At the end we had over twenty-one thousand irrigated acres in Warner Valley, something beyond another million acres of BLM rangeland leased, and we ran around six thousand fine mother cows.

Warner was more for my father. He had been to classes in engineering at the College of Agricultural Science in Corvallis; my father was one of the new men, a visionary; he saw possibilities.

In 1936 he bought a cable-drum Caterpillar RD-6 track layer fitted out with a dozer blade, which he used to start building a seventeen-mile diversion levee to carry the spring flood waters of Twenty Mile

Creek north along the east side of the valley, past our swamplands. Seventeen miles. In those times such a project was considered insanely ambitious—literally.

My father was the joke of the country, but not for long. He jerry-rigged a generator and battery system to run off the diesel engine of that RD-6, mounted it with lights, and ran it at the levee-building twenty-four hours a day, summer and winter, except for fuel stops and maintenance. In 1937 he bought an RD-7 and used it to build his levee while he started plowing the tule beds with the RD-6, also twenty-four hours a day.

Near as I can fix them, from conversations with my mother, my next memories come from the summer of the following year, 1938, the year I was six and scheduled to start school in the fall. By that time my father had already taken a bumper crop of oats off the several hundred acres broken

Alfalfa field just cut and baled, Double J. A. Land & Livestock, Smith Valley Ranch, Nevada

out into so-called plow ground, and my mother was working as his bookkeeper and factotum. One of her duties involved driving out to cross the natural drainage on the east side of the valley at a place called the Beatty Bridge. Then she would head south through the greasewood wastelands just above the edges of the swamps, to a cluster of abandoned ramshackle homesteader buildings, a house and sheds known as the Fee Place, where my father had established his farming and catskinners camp and cookhouse. My mother had to make the run every couple of days, carrying spare parts and groceries, and she often took me with her.

It was summer and hot, but my mother would stop after we came off the Beatty Bridge and roll up all the windows. Then she would rev the engine on the old black Buick she drove to her work, sweat already accumulating on her upper lip, and we would plunge off into the alkali dust, which would rise around us like something alive from that deeply eroded roadway through the greasewood. My mother drove that road fast, holding her breath, as if speed were a way of escape, and the long rooster tail of dust we raised hung visible in the morning air for a half hour after we had passed. Down there in our Buick, that part of the trip was like a passage through darkness for me, and, I'm sure, for my mother. The fine dust sifted inside the Buick, no matter how tightly it was sealed, like water that might drown us, alive as it hung in the light.

Demonic seems the operative word. Then we would come out onto the rocky shale of the slight rise to the Fee Point where those old buildings stood, and the air would clear, and we would be safe for awhile, until we had to start back. We would roll down the windows, and the dust would sift away off the windshield, and my mother would lick her upper lip, and again I would realize how childish I had been, frightened of dust.

The high ground at Fee Point had been an old camping ground for the Paiutes and Modocs and Klamaths. They must have camped there hundreds of times over centuries, hunting the water birds and gathering native grains from the swamps. My mother would banter with some camp cook, the only one I remember being a sour-smelling young woman named Ida, and drink her couple of cups of coffee, and I would hunt the high ground on the Fee Point for arrowheads, which I found by the pocketful.

But what I most vividly recall from those early trips to the Fee Place was standing on the high ground and looking out across the raw sixteen-foot berm of earth that was the diversion levee as it curled around the high ground at Fee Point, and looking beyond the levee to the plow ground, where drill rows of my father's oat crop were emerging from the earth.

My mother and that camp cook named Ida, both of them in thin summery yellow dresses, their arms bare in the sunlight, came out to stand below me, shading their eyes and gazing in the direction I was looking, looking to one another and talking and nodding. There is no imagining what they might have been looking toward as they stood—or as they now stand, blessing this memory of the degree to which we all believed in one another in those days.

In late summer, before the harvest, my father would take me and my younger brother and sister with him to see his oat fields and let us run through the heavy crop, beating trails of hide-and-seek like little animals, the seed heads twisted and gathered over our heads. In those years, on that new ground, we raised the heaviest oats anywhere in America, my father tells me, according to what buyers told him. No doubt it was a common phenomenon in those years. Somebody somewhere was always breaking out new ground, and for a couple of years their crops were the finest anywhere in America. I vividly recall crouching out in the oat fields, hidden, and looking up to see nothing but sky beyond the bright stalks and the dangling, spiked seed heads.

In all this life we had there was still a kind of Western readiness and wildness. My mother was working for the Ford dealer in Klamath Falls when she met my father. She says he came in disheveled and un- shaven and obviously hungover after a poker game of several days' duration, thirty- one years old and never married or close to it. He tossed out a wadded pocketful of folding money he'd won and told her he wanted a Ford, right away. "Well," she said, "a man like that caught your eye."

My father continued to run at life in that heedless way, much to the conster- nation of my grandfather, but the work got done. A man with an almost infinite capacity for loyalty, my father kept his friends from the old days around him, working, and cut them in on the action—much as he could.

Once in those childhood days he took me riding the levee bank roads with him in late May, to admire the drill rows of crops, and we came across a hundred-and-some- acre plot of seeded ground that had been reflooded with creek water to the depth of about a foot and a half. Some headgate had been opened by mistake, drowning the crop, a rather expensive mistake.

An old Jeep pickup was coming toward us, driven by a man named Louie Hanson, who had worked on and off as a catskinner and mechanic for my father from the be- ginning. Louie was on a lifetime drunk, and some time in the last couple of days he had opened the wrong headgate and flooded the field before us.

Louie pulled his Jeep up beside my father's pickup, rolled down the window, and faced the music with a wide, shit-eating grin. "Well, hell, Oscar," he said, "sometimes you get drunk."

"That's right, Louie," my father said. "But sometimes I sober up."

That was it. They both drove off. My grandfather wanted old Louie run off the ranch, but my father would hear none of it. Many years later Louie Hanson died while working for us; he had given us a lifetime, with damned little coming back to him beyond a room in the bunkhouse and board and subsistence wages. My father is legendary for the good regard paid him by other men; nobody ever doubted he was honest and would treat you decently as you deserved, and maybe better.

In the later years there were serious divi- sions in our family, springing from a central disagreement about the economic relation- ship between the cattle ranching side of our operation, and what was called "the farming." The argument seemed more than anything to concern itself with matters of style; some of us were cowboys, and some of us were farmers. Truth is, after a heyday of big grain prices during World War II, our farming ended up designed to support the cow business my grandfather saw as fun- damental.

In the war years, as my father's cat- skinners brought more and more of the

Bill
Trampe and Don Rundell stacking
hay onto a wagon for feeding at the
Trampe Ranches, Gunnison,
Colorado

swampland under drainage and the plow, the economics of our agriculture swung heavily on the profits from farming. And what money was left after paying the notes was supposed to go back into the property. Most of it did, after my father outraged my grandfather by buying into a couple of race horses.

Over the years we bought another three of those D-7 Caterpillar tractors and kept them busy; the seventeen-mile diversion canal was finished; we bought four John Deere 36 combines with eighteen-foot headers; inside the diversion canal we built a network of drainage ditches and redwood headgates; the shallow lakes were pumped dry, huge fields were marked off, 750 acres in Huston Swamp, 800 acres in Dodson Lake. The headgates were opened when

the spring runoff waters came, and those fields were flood irrigated and pumped dry again. We were reinventing the land and the water-flow patterns of the valley on a model copied from industry, irrevocably altering the ecology of everything, including our own lives. We were also making an irrevocable move toward the world of technology.

In the spring of 1946, with the war ended, came another simple and enormous change. We started putting up the loose hay on our thousands of acres of wild meadow with tractors, and it wasn't many years before most of the matched work teams were gone off to chicken feed. Their harnesses hung on pegs in the barns and rotted there.

The haying had traditionally worked

huge crews through the months of summer. What was known as "the mow crew" ran around thirty mowing machines and twenty dump rakes, which translates into more than fifty men, some working, some coming, some going, and maybe two hundred head of work horses. Two stacking crews of around ten men each followed the mowing after a week or so of letting the hay cure on the ground, dragging the buckloads of hay up over the beaver slides into hundred-ton stacks, one every half a day when they were up to speed.

What it came to, as these crews and their cooks moved around the valley from hay camp to hay camp, was a place inhabited by productive life. You could look out over the valley in the morning and see the strings of dust rising to clean sky over those hay camp corrals, dust stirred up by the circling horses, as those crews caught their teams. And you could think: This is the right dream, America as Thomas Jefferson had imagined it, as it was supposed to be—before everything went to tractors and down the road to agribusiness.

In 1949 I left for eight years, majoring in general agriculture at Oregon State and then working in Air Force photo intelligence. When I came back to the ranch, I found myself in a new world. Paved roads and electricity and television had come to the valley. And we were working toward perfection of the fields. If I had known anything about my own mind, I would have found a way to leave again, right then, and not ten years later, after so much was ruined.

Big round
bales of hay being fed in winter; this
equipment was designed exclusively
for this size bale.

Hay meadows
at the Noffsinger Ranches, Walden,
Colorado

Stacking
and shipping bales of alfalfa hay in
North Park, Colorado

Cutting
a hay crop, Noffsinger Ranches,
Walden, Colorado
opposite

But, no, for a long time I loved it. We all did; for a long time we thought we were doing the great good work, remaking the world according to an image borrowed from efficiency experts.

The old animal-centered agricultural world I had grown up in was mostly gone— just like that, after centuries—and now I congratulate myself on having lived in it at the end. The ranch was being turned into a machine for feeding livestock. The swamps were drained, and the thronging flocks of hundreds of thousands of water birds were diminishing most every year. The hunting was still fine, if you had never seen anything else. But we knew. Our irrigation system was a masterpiece of complexity, with over five thousand water-control devices, head-gates, valves, eighteen-inch pumps. We could run the water around and around in that system on a dry year, pumping it back up to irrigate with again—until, so the joke went, it wore out. For a number of years the main part of my work in the spring was that system, a twenty-four-hour-a-day job called balancing water.

We had leveled a couple of thousand acres for alfalfa, and we kept leveling more. For eight years after the death of my grandfather I was the farming boss at the MC, in my father's footsteps, running an operation we had always—since my father's early days—called the grain camp. And I loved it. Those crops and that irrigation system were the finest playthings of my life. We were making something perfect as it could be in our notion of the world, inscribing our vision on the earth and in the seasons like artists, and the making *was* an art. Do not mistake it, the impulse that drove us to work was as much toward a vision of agricultural perfection as it was economic. We were doing God's work and

making a sacred place on the earth.

Except it didn't work; not at all, really. In the long run it collapsed back on itself. That seventeen-mile outside diversion levee my father had built in the 1930s washed out in the early 1960s, and we rebuilt it all, pushing the levee up until it was invulnerable. After that the spring floods were never much threat. We cut our alfalfa and tame hay with swathers, followed by five-wire balers, and harrow beds to pick up the bales from the field and stack them mechanically. We sprayed our crops with 2-4-D Ethyl and Malathion, and even Parathion for clover mite in the barley—and we shortened our own lives. We baited the coyotes with 1080, and rodents destroyed our alfalfa. We irrigated and reirrigated, pumped and drained, and our rich peat soil started to go saline.

We couldn't hire anybody who cared enough about our mechanical work to do it right. The old men, like Louie Hanson, who had started out with my father in the 1930s, were dying. It was a rare season in the bunkhouse when some old man didn't turn up dead for breakfast. That will break your heart. And not many young men were coming to the work with much beyond disdain. The men who hired out for ranch work in the 1960s were missing the boat, and they knew it. They despised themselves for it. And thus they despised the work.

And up on the hill, above the old buckaroo camp, there was the industrial plant we called the feed mill, an impressive collection of steel buildings, with rollers and grinders and blowers and chain drives and augers and hundred-horsepower electric motors, a huge grain storage bunker, and an endlessness of lots for fattening cattle. By the end we had built lots enough to hold most of our cow herd; we shipped toward five thousand fat cattle every year. The mill was designed to chop hay and roll grains and mix in additives from molasses to growth-inducing chemicals like Stilbestoral, a howling, stinking place where the work proceeded at the pace of the machinery. In winter those thousands of animals penned into that lot, waiting for the feed truck to come down the aisle and for eventual slaughter, were only another adjunct to that feed mill. In spring we cleaned the manure from the lots with those D-7 Caterpillars. Our dream had led us to these processes, and that work seemed demonic and hateful as we did it.

I don't want what I'm saying here to be taken as the sentimentalities of a man looking back on the paradise of a lost world from childhood. My boyhood on that ranch was most often a hard, scab-handed affair that left me yearning for the civilities of my school-year life in town. But it was a life conducted on a human scale on a natural, ecologically functional landscape we understood as more than a machine for agricultural productivity. We followed the dream of machinelike industrial perfection we had been given, a Corps of Engineers/Ag School mirage of remaking the world in our own image.

And it didn't work, not at all, for both practical and spiritual reasons.

The ecology of our valley was complex beyond our understanding, and it simply began to die as we went on manipulating it in ever more frantic ways. As it was dead and empty of the old natural life, it became a place where no one wanted to live. In our right minds we want to live in places that smell of life, not of agricultural chemicals.

We are talking about a social phenom-

enon, a drive to industrialize that soured and undercut the value of what drew most people to ranching in the first place. God knows, we used to say, nobody but a fool would go into the cow business if they had it in mind to get rich. You'd be a hundred times better off, economically, with your money in a string of shoe stores or Dairy Queens. So it is enormously heartening, in recent years, to find signs, however meager, of backlash.

The old desert cow outfits in northern Nevada are going back to horse-drawn chuck wagons, for economic reasons, so they say, and I'm sure they are right. A four-wheel-drive outfit is going to cost you money right down the line, so many thousands of dollars when it comes shiny new off the lot, and then there are brake linings and drive-line bearings and broken axles

Black Angus
cattle grazing, Beaver Meadows
Ranch, McLeod, Montana
top

Ranchers
still feed the old way, especially
in the deep-snow country of the
William Van Valkenberg Ranch,
Walden, Colorado.

and carburator kits and belted radial tires and all the rest. Those horses keep on grass and hay.

And there are other motives for going back to the horses and some approximation of the old life. Maybe in the long run they are economic, too. What it comes down to is rediscovering reasons for doing the work.

Call it reconnecting to the sacred; in any event, it is recognition that you are eager to live connected to a specific place and its seasons, with a run of territory, eastern Oregon or West Texas or wherever, and live intimately with the animals that happen to inhabit that country, creature to creature. We all yearn for connection to such a living world and for significant work, like raising food, a way of living so unlike that perfectly alienating factory-land daydream of efficiency called agribusiness.

People stick to ranching because they love the feel of a quick little horse moving intently after cattle, or maybe the smell of greasewood after summer rain or new-cut alfalfa on a spring morning, or the stretch of damp rawhide as they work at braiding a riata, or the look of a mother cow as she trails her dusty way back to her calf after a long walk to water. People stick to ranching because they love the feel and smell and sound of things, and because they share those mostly unspoken loves with other people they can trust as somewhere near to decent.

All over the West, just recently, cowboys and ranch women and farm hands and sheepherders have been gathering to declaim their verse to one another. Such gatherings are raunchy and loud and finally quite heartbreaking in their openness and intimacy, once all the media hype and macho nonsense have slipped aside. The gatherings are the other side of that bloody-

knuckled coin that is rodeo, and they are open celebrations of things ranchland people respect and care about most deeply— the land they have chosen to live on, their work, and, at center, one another, this companionship.

As the economics of ranching deteriorate, our good people seem driven to opening out, and we can all take heart from their willingness to have a try at naming those things they take to be sacred. You don't hear many poems about feed mills. I think of my mother's piano, the strings popping and twanging in that wreck so many years ago. She hated the stiff-lipped silences so commonplace in my father's family as they drove themselves toward the finally sad thing they took as success, and she left the ranching life a long time ago. Maybe she would be happier now.

Moving horses to winter range during the Sombrero Ranch horse drive, Colorado

LIVESTOCK

BAXTER BLACK

The range cow is the blue-collar worker of the wild and woolly West. In real life, as in the movies, she is the essential prop. Would pioneers have braved the mountains of Colorado, the deserts of Arizona, or the blizzards of Montana to plant corn? No! The range cow has never sought top billing in her supporting role. She has plodded, milled, and stampeded over the vast western landscape like the perennial graduate student, unaware of her destination and ambivalent about getting there.

How did she get where she is today? She walked. She walked for millions of miles and millions of cow years. She is still walking, tracing the trails her four-legged forerunners have worn smooth over three centuries. In the chronology of the settling of the West by peripatetic Europeans, she came somewhere after the trappers and before white women. Which just about makes her a native.

The modern range cow is to the pure-bred bovine dam as the five-hundred-dollar-a-month cowboy is to the Madison Avenue executive. They have nothing in common, save some fundamental anatomical coincidences. Although her physical appearance has changed with time, her attitude remains surly and unsocial, at best. Self-improvement courses are not her bag. You could no more walk up to a range cow than you could an elk or a discount-store employee. They are domesticated, not tamed.

To make it perfectly clear, the heroine of this chapter is the range cow. Not the herculean bull with family jewels that hang

The natural curiosity of ranch horses, Boettcher Ranch, Walden, Colorado

like counterweights to his mountainous head. Nor the noble horse, whose journeyman work has secured his place in Western lore. Not even the faithful dog, the clever coyote, or the broken-mouth ewe, all of whom appear in cameo roles.

In cowboy parlance, those of her kind are referred to as commercial, grade, or stock cows. They can be described loosely as Herefords, blacks, and black ballys. They are descendants of Hereford and Aberdeen

Angus forebears who emigrated from Great Britain during the nineteenth century. The harsh environment, the demand for choice beef, and the occasional infusion of Longhorn spermatozoa have distilled them to their present state.

The Hereford cow is the matriarch of the modern cow business. After Longhorn cattle settled the West and served their purpose, ranchers began importing quality Herefords. These hardy white-face cattle proliferated, depositing their genes among less distinguished critters. As the years rolled by, the influence of these bluebloods spread like cheap burgundy on a white tuxedo. Soon cows that had the conformation of a backyard swing set bore a strong color resemblance to the red-bodied, white-faced Hereford. The continued introduction of purebred Hereford bulls into this duke's mixture of cows inexorably bred a better cow. She inherited the bearing and appearance of upper-crust bovine royalty, but she retained the commoner's ability to hustle and survive. Like a princess who can shoot a mean game of eight ball, she didn't take herself too seriously.

Commercial cattlemen sought to improve their herds. By the early 1900s the black Angus began to make his presence known. He came into the game armed with three unique plays. He threw polled (hornless) calves and claimed that his offspring had a lower birth weight. These first two selling points gained him entrance into many a ranch. The third play did not become apparent until feedlot management became sophisticated. Black cattle matured earlier and, as a result, fattened quicker.

An Angus bull bred to a Hereford cow produces a black bally calf. The calf has a color pattern like a Hereford, except where the Hereford was red, the crossbred off-

A newborn calf is licked clean and dry by her mother.

Angus bull
covered with icicles, Big Horn Ranch,
Cowdrey, Colorado

〜〜〜〜

Cross-bred calf (left photo) and Black Angus cow with cross-bred white-face calf and Hereford cow drinking water through the ice (right photo), Big Horn Ranch, Cowdrey, Colorado

spring is black. It's like a black-and-white photo of a Hereford—usually polled. Black ballys (pronounced as in baldface lie, Lucille Ball, and balderdash) possessed a significant asset, one any seed corn producer could have easily predicted: hybrid vigor.

The first-cross offspring of two different pure breeds grew bigger and faster than offspring produced within the same breed. A black bally heifer combined the good mothering and foraging traits of the Hereford with the fattening ability and resistance to eye disease of the Angus. So she was valued as a herd-replacement cow. When she was bred back to a purebred Angus or Hereford bull, her offspring was no longer a first cross, and the hybrid vigor diminished. Although geneticists were disappointed, this phenomenon was comforting

to the suppliers of purebred breeding stock and allowed the growth-promotant industry to proliferate.

Second-cross calves and beyond also lose their predictable appearance. Their color or markings can look like tie-dyed spaghetti: brockle-face, baldface, solid, red-neck cattle in red or black with white frosting.

Herefords, blacks, and black ballys still comprise the majority of the standard-issue range cows. However, I have never seen a rancher cull a roan cow, that less visible descendant of the shorthorn breed.

Draw a line from Fresno to Atlanta. South of this imaginary latitude, known as the Little Ear Parallel (so named because cattle with Zebu ancestry are said to have "a little ear"—which is a paradox, since

these cattle have ears like a fruit bat's. But such is the logic of cowboys), the influence of *Bos indicus* becomes overwhelming. The Brahma (rhymes with tamer, as in lion tamer) range cow is king. From the mosquito- and tick-infested palmetto swamps of Florida to the 120-degree blow-sand filaree of the Arizona desert, no breed can compete. Her predecessors first appeared on the Gulf coast in the mid 1800s, having arrived from India and Brazil. They were not stowaways, but were deliberately imported because of their resistance to the effects of hot weather.

There are some striking differences between the British breeds (like the Herefords and Angus) and brahman cattle, not the least of which is personality. Brahman cows are fierce protectors of their young and do not voluntarily allow their being handled. Otherwise, when shown the proper respect, they are gentle, benevolent critters around humans. They do have one rather disconcerting trait: they have no fear of cowboys. The Hereford bull or Angus cow may charge a man. They may bellow and paw the ground if egged on. But most of their ferocity is bluster. Given any choice, they will usually run. Not so the agitated Brahma. You stand there with your broken plastic whip, waving your arms and shouting obscenities at the cow. She looks you level in the eye and says, "Hey, fool. Look around! You're a long way from the house."

A great deal of effort has been made to take advantage of Brahman traits by British and continental breed producers. The Brahma has been crossed successfully with the Shorthorn (Santa Gertrudis), Hereford (Beefmaster), Angus (Brangus), Simmental (Simbra), Limousin (Brahmousin), Charolais (Charbray), and Salers (Bralers), as well as others. Probably the most successful

Cattle grazing
on the Van Deusen Ranch,
Emmett, Idaho

cross has been the Bramoco, a cross between cattle ranching and the oil business. As one of my Texas friends pointed out, "The best way to raise cattle is in the shade ... the shade of an oil well."

The last half of the twentieth century has brought major changes to the North American cattle industry, many due to the influence of what are loosely called "exotic breeds." For the most part, they are well-established European breeds that have been imported to cross with the American range cow. These breeds promise higher perform-ance, leather upholstery, and four-on-the-floor. Their number and variety are surpassed only by the number and variety of new automobiles unleashed on the public every fall. They go by such names as Charlois, Simmental, Limousin, Salers, Tarentaise,

Chianina, Gelbvieh, Blonde d'Aquitaine, Maine-Anjou, Pinzgauer, and Piedmontese, and they are steadily integrating themselves into the genetic pool of the range-cow herd. Yellow, orange, burgundy, and blue cows appear sprinkled amid the traditional red, white, and black. Their influence is limited only by cost and availability.

An overview of the range-cow herds would not be complete without paying homage to the Longhorn. Brought by the conquering Spaniards, Longhorns were the dominant breed on the western ranges for two centuries. They were distinguished by their long horns and hardiness.

By 1900 the Herefords were taking over, and the Longhorn population declined rapidly for decades until the breed became an object of curiosity. Then in the 1960s,

Braford
cattle—cross of Brahma and
Hereford—on the Bandana Ranch,
Baker, Oregon

the cattle business became more specialized and more scientific. Seminarians, consultants, and academics had computerized, analyzed, and proselytized the beef industry. By reviewing performance records, environmental data, lineage, and nutrition, they could evaluate a cow without ever seeing her. This struck a false chord in the heart of many a die-hard cowman, and the Longhorn was reincarnated. With her varied colors and majestic horns, she stands as a symbol of the cow business before it became hi-tech. It is still possible to see Longhorns grazing between some rancher's house and the road. He keeps them there to remind us all not to lose sight of the original model. Like Washington's picture on the dollar.

To understand the range cow, it is appropriate to engage in some speculative psychoanalysis. Whoever named the Dumb Friends League must have punched a few cows. They have an IQ somewhere between the sandhill crane and a creosote post. You cannot reason with a cow. A sure sign of vestigial intelligence would be the ability to learn something. You may have noticed the dearth of trained cow acts, seeing-eye cows, or cow obedience courses.

The chicken has made two significant contributions to the world: the chicken-fried steak and the pecking order. A pecking order is the controlling factor in a cow's life. It determines were she eats, how well she eats, where she sleeps, her place by the windmill tank, on the trail, in the truck, and at the table. Her position in this scruffy hierarchy is not a function of beauty, size, family history, age, or S.A.T. score. The cow

YO Ranch
Longhorn cow and calf

Baby-sitter cow: one cow "baby sits" while others go off for feed or water; each day a different cow will look after a group of calves, C S Ranch, Cimarron, New Mexico

with the dominant *will* ascends the throne.

Maternal instinct is strong in a cow, though it varies with breeds and individuals. One of the continually amazing sights is to watch 275 calves after a branding turned back with their mammas. The cows and calves mill and bawl until each is paired up. It's been pointed out to me that 275 mothers could be turned loose in a gym full of kindergarten children, and they would pair up likewise. But it's still a wondrous sight.

Cow motherhood extends to protecting her young against well-meaning cowboys. Many a cowboy has been hurt doctoring a sick calf when he turned his back on mamma.

Dealing with range cows everyday is not a job for the squeamish, the vacillating, the short-winded, or the fastidious. One must be able to out-think a thousand-pound brute that has the intellect of a Bartlett pear. Fortunately, most cowmen I know are equal to the challenge. They possess that unique essential quality: cow savvy.

Black bally
cow "talking" to her calf; calves are
separated from their mothers for the
first time to brand them

Black Angus
cow "mothering up"—identifying her
calf, Big Creek Ranch, Encampment,
Wyoming

Unassisted live birth on a frozen meadow, Big Horn Ranch, Cowdrey, Colorado: The calf's head appears first, still within the amniotic sac; the calf is pushed out during contractions and is born. The mother immediately gets up and turns to start licking the calf clean—which serves to dry, massage, and warm the calf, and to promote bonding; cows are very protective and tender mothers. Shortly, the calf will get up and start to nurse.

Grafting is a method of "fooling" a cow into mothering a calf that is not her own. It is used when an orphan calf needs a mother, or when twins are born (cows tend not to be able to mother two calves at the same time), or when for some other reason a calf's birth mother does not provide adequate care. Grafting requires a mother cow whose own calf was stillborn or has died shortly after birth. Here, Bill Trampe drags such a calf; its mother follows. She will be put in a barn stall while the dead calf is skinned from its front shoulders to under the tail. Leaving the tail intact is important so that when the skin is placed on a healthy calf, the cow will think it is her original calf.

The skin is fitted with baling twine to attach it to the new calf.

In this case, luckily, twin calves were born to another cow the same night. Since it is better to have only one calf per cow, the smaller twin calf was used for this graft. The twins were separated from their mother overnight and held in a wooden box warmed with heat lamps until morning, when the grafting was done. Often, when a cow loses a calf, there is not an extra calf to graft, so the cow is allowed to dry up.

The new calf, fitted with skin, is put into a corral to await the introduction to the cow, which is fooled into thinking this is her original calf and accepts it as her own. Within a few days the skin will dry up and fall off; by then she will know "her" calf well.

Band of sheep
trailing north in western Nevada

While ranchers have proudly pasted pictures of cattle into the historical scrapbook of the West, sheep have blithely continued to survive in the background. Though their numbers have declined significantly under the steamroller of polyester, they remain an active part of the livestock economy.

Sheep ranching in the West is vastly different from midwestern and eastern flocks. In the East flocks number less than a hundred, while in the West sheep are run in bands varying in size from six hundred to two thousand head, depending on the season. A band is divided into two or three bunches looked after by a herder who, with his dogs, keeps them trailing to greener pastures. Usually, the bands are moved from winter to summer range and back. Lambing out on the range was common until coyotes gained a modicum of congressional protection. Since then many sheep operations bring their pregnant ewes to the safety of the lambing sheds.

Range ewes are white-face, fine-wool

animals of Rambouillet and Debouillet ancestry. In each band 90 percent of the breeding bucks are black-face (Suffolk). The remaining 10 percent are white-face. The female offspring of these white-face bucks are saved as replacement ewes. The black-face-cross lambs are shipped to market.

Sheep are much maligned. They are often spoken of as weak, stupid, helpless, prone to catastrophe, and odoriferous. It has been my experience that sheep are like cats: they are so hardy you never know they're sick until it's too late to treat them. The most telling comment about sheep spoken by many a rancher—only slightly tongue in cheek—is, "I run cattle to keep my self-respect and raise sheep to pay the bills."

The ranch horse is the cowboy's companion and tool—somewhere between a teddy bear and a good pocket knife. It's not quite the same romantic relationship that movies portray. Trigger and Silver were well-groomed, well-mannered sidekicks that served as spouse substitutes for Roy and the Ranger. Working cowboys are polygamous. They ride two or three horses on a ranch. Often, one is their favorite, but it's more like a marriage after the honeymoon is over.

As a rule, cowboys admire good horse-

Range ewe with newborn twin lambs; twins are common in sheep

flesh, but looks don't make a horse. Which explains why you see so many big-footed, long-legged sloggers with a pendulous lip and a head like a chest of drawers. As with cowboys, they may not look like much, but they're good at what they do.

Saddle horses come from various places. A few of the big outfits will run a band of brood mares. The colts are branded as yearlings. They are castrated and docked coming two years old and broke or sold shortly after. In the days of running mustangs, a few young colts were caught and made into saddle horses. Nowadays, most ranches buy their horses saddle-broke from neighbors, auction barns, or horse traders.

To my way of thinking, there are two kinds of people. Those who are comfortable with horses and those who aren't (and the latter group does include some cowboys). There are ten-year-old kids who can make a horse do wheelies, and people who've ridden for fifty years who still can't tell if a horse is limping.

Breaking a horse involves dominating his spirit. It can be done with force or with kindness. Done properly, either approach is effective. In the wild, horses are social animals. Each has a specific position within the band. Like corporate middle management or schoolyard rank, each pair of horses meets face to face and determines which is higher on the totem pole. It is usually a non-violent confrontation. When one horse and one man square off, the same thing occurs. The horse has an obvious advantage. There is no way a 160-pound soft-shelled human with smashable appendages and bipedal awkwardness can physically best a 1,200-pound bundle of nerve and muscle shaped like a horse.

The horse must be conquered psychologically.

Riding a bronc until he'll pull a plow is one way. The other involves giving the horse a choice. He allows you to have your way with him, or you make him uncomfortable. This can be done with one-leg hobbles, lip chains, whips, loud voices, side lines, sacks, kind words, gentle handling, firm retribution, and understanding.

First thing I do when I meet a horse is get acquainted—let him smell me; I scratch his face, talk to him, assure him I'm not going to hurt him. Horses that have been handled roughly, eared down, hit, or jerked on, actually sigh with relief when they realize they're in no danger. As simple as that sounds, that little effort on my part often is all that's needed to establish my dominance.

Of course, it's not always that easy. There are horses I've had to rope and throw to even touch their face.

On the ranch, breakin' the new horses is usually one man's responsibility. He's the one that is described by all as "a good hand with a horse." He might be a less than credible cowperson, but he can read a horse's mind. They are not boisterous men. They have a reserved, easy style and are persistent in their dealing with horses or other humans.

It would be fair to say that cowboys are lucky that God invented the horse. Handling range cows would be a far more difficult task on foot.

No chapter on livestock would be complete without a word about cow dogs. Westerners in the sheep business have bred and trained stock dogs for generations. These shelties, shepherds, and collies are a marvel to watch.

Quarter Horse mare communicating with her foal, R. A. Brown Ranch, Throckmorton, Texas

They perform their master's wishes by following subtle verbal or visual commands. Combined with instinct, this makes them a furry extension of the herder's thoughts.

However, there is a difference between sheepmen and cowmen. Allowing that there are some splendid, cow dogs that ride around in the back of the occasional cowboy's pickup, they are the exception.

The common cow dog is represented by that noble canine companion and head of ranch security, the Blue Heeler. They are singularly endowed with a good livestock instinct, a deep sense of loyalty, and the stubborness of an IRS auditor. It's been my observation that cowmen are not the most patient humans on earth with their dogs. So dog training is sporadic at best.

At any cow-working in the West, the neighbors all show up to help. They bring their dogs. These dogs leap out and commence to fight with each other for two hours. Then they spend the rest of the day under your feet or in the gate. The most common command I hear echoing out the corrals is "Go git in the pickup, you sunnuvabitch!"

The Code of the West prevents a good cowboy from criticizing another man's dog . . . so I'll quit here.

Sombrero
Ranch horses after the first day of a horse drive, Maybell, Colorado

Big
Creek Ranch horses

COWBOY ART BETWEEN THE LINES

H A L   C A N N O N

The most memorable moments in the life of the American cowboy are those that pass unnoticed— the frostbitten day in the saddle, the long hours working with a calving cow in labor, a summer day on the desert without water. Every cowboy poem, song, story, or drawing is merely an echo of serendipitous events, poignant moments, translated into a few well-chosen words or lines on paper. Even the best of the cowboy's artistic expressions can only hint at the reality of the working life. And it's therefore impossible to explain just why an occupation as hard and humble as cowboying has taken on such mythic proportions in American life. But the history of the cowboy and his relationship with American popular culture tells us part of the story.

Early in this century, folklorists like John Lomax took notice of the working and social lives of cowboys and began recording the words to the poems they recited and the songs they sang. During the same period, fueled by an interest in the West engendered by dime novels and even a few two-bit ones, like Owen Wister's *The Virginian* (1902), others began a fuller documentation of the cowboy. His dress, gear, and working environment were portrayed by painters, while novelists and journalists took notice of his language, beliefs, values, and stories. A romantic myth soon permeated American consciousness, yet it is notable that very little of the cowboy's true work was portrayed. As someone said of Wister's novel, there were a lot of cowboys and horses,

Horse in a trailer on a freezing day in Colorado

but scarcely a cow in the book. Further, with the exception of Will James, Andy Adams, N. Howard "Jack" Thorp, and a few others, all of these descriptions were the productions of outsiders, who didn't understand the year-round cycle of work or the itinerant lives of their subjects. But now, with John Wayne and Tom Mix gone and only a few of the old Hollywood cowboys still in the saddle, we have begun to look at the occupation itself, as described by its professionals.

That is not to say that there has been no interplay between the art of the profession and art about the profession. Even the most hard-bitten puncher is capable of seeing the romance inherent in his life, different as that may be from Hollywood's confections. It's an occupation constantly changing, maybe fading a little, ever more reliant on machines and technology, and so seen nostalgically even by the greenest hands. The truth is that there has always been a certain vanity and pride that is expressed in the clothes and gear and language, too. Further, though cowboys are always the most critical of authenticity in the way they are portrayed, they take deep pride in the tradition of being shown in a romantic light. When they are not portrayed this way, they get angry. A case in point is the portrayal of the so-called urban cowboy, which provoked little affection from practicing cowboys.

How has the cowboy, the working cowboy, described and expressed his own life? Interpretations by outsiders have been piled so thick and deep that the cowboy's

own version of the significance of his life has all but been lost. Cowboys rarely have agents in New York to get their words out. Working cowboy artists have little access to prestigious galleries to show their work. Then how do you find the real stuff of cowboys, the stuff that reflects the work and the life as well as the costume and heroic saga?

At ranches.

Ranches are where cowboys work and where you find the heart of their expressive culture. There the oral narratives, the vivid language, the poetry, the music, the craft and art of cowboys abound for those who know how to find it. These expressions are complex, coded with terminology and detail known only to insiders. The existence of this rich welter of expression belies another false assumption: that the only worthwhile cowboy art is that which is made accessible to the general public, simplified, introduced, explained. In fact, the best cowboy poems, drawings, and crafts depend on fine details and subtle points that can appeal only to those in the life, those who share the dream, those who can read between the lines.

The existence of these long-held and deeply felt traditions of verbal, literary, and visual arts and of decorative crafts suggests the depth of commitment of their practitioners. Even if many of the tasks of this life are tedious and frustrating, even if many people in the occupation don't have university degrees or formal training, that doesn't mean—as some critics maintain—that cowboys themselves can't find romance in their lives or that they can't possibly develop skills as writers, singers, lecturers, illustrators, craftsmen, or plain thinkers.

I have noticed that when journalists write stories about cowboys they often get stopped by the vernacular of cowboy speech. Rather than quoting the precision and beauty of cowboys' talk, they dwell on language that makes the cowboy sound stupid. In a recent copy of the *Federation Review* I wrote about the wisdom of spending public money to allow cowboys to express their thoughts through the artistic tradition of poetry. I even suggested that one did not necessarily need a Ph.D. or a facility for polysyllabic words to express the deeper aspects of what it is to be human. I heard nothing from my scholarly colleagues after the article was published until the next issue of the *Review* appeared containing a reply from another Harold Cannon, a proper Englishman who works at the National Endowment for the Humanities. He didn't want anyone to think that *he* might have written such blasphemy. In his letter he states, "Cowboy poets, indeed! Almost as farfetched as that other famous hoax, Matthew Arnold and his Scholar Gypsy!"

Trailing a
single cow requires time and
patience.

There is a long tradition of working cowboys writing and reciting poetry about their lives. Working cowboys such as D. J. O'Malley began writing poems for local stockmen's periodicals in the 1880s. By 1910 at least ten books of cowboy poetry had been published, poetry that was reminiscent—in form if not in content—of the rhymed, ballad-meter folk poetry of the British Isles, poetry with medieval roots embedded firmly in oral tradition. This poetry not only contained artful views of cowboy life, but also spoke to contemporary issues relating to the occupation. In a way, cowboy poetry served to promote a kind of worker solidarity in the context of Western individualism. By the mid twenties, cowboy and rancher poets had begun self-publishing, finding a market for their poems at events such as the commercial rodeo, which was just then getting its start. Well-known poet Curley Fletcher published an inexpensive booklet of his verse in 1917 and sold it at rodeos where he was performing as a trick rider. That is how his poem "The Strawberry Roan" gained entry into the vast folk repertoire.

Among cowboy poets, there were great differences in occupation and economic status. Badger Clark, later named poet laureate of South Dakota, grew up on ranches. He eventually became a popular lecturer on the Chautauqua circuit and at college campuses around the West, as did the folklorist and collector of song, John Lomax. Bruce Kiskaddon, on the other hand, published at his own expense a popular book while he was a working cowboy in 1924. A year later he quit the cowboy life to go to Hollywood and drive chariots in the first film version of *Ben Hur.* He stayed on in Southern California, spending the rest of his life as a bellhop in Los Angeles hotels.

Yet he remained a cowboy poet by writing a monthly poem for *Western Livestock* and by publishing three other books before his death in 1950. All of these men profoundly influenced the development of cowboy poetry. Their work was read, admired, and embraced by cowboys and ranchers of their day, and eventually the poems were learned

Mike McClellan is a "day-work" cowboy for the Moorhouse Ranch during branding—which means that he hires on by the day.

BETWEEN THE LINES

There's something I'm not forgetting,
But it's something I could not say.
I could not arrange the setting
And the scene, in the proper way.
The air of the desert and mountain,
The smoke of the far out camp,
The whispering voice of the night wind
And the picketed horse's tramp.
The tread of the moving cattle,
The song that the riders croon,
The swing and the sway of the saddle
That goes to the lilt of the tune.
The race after wild young horses
That beats any hunt for game;
The battle of wits and forces
Until the wild brutes are tame.
For the strong young steeds are fighters
That are raised on the hills and plains,
They must learn to balance their riders;
You must teach them to answer the reins.
It calls for skillful riders,
Your hardiest strongest men;
The buck and bawl, the sickening fall,
And the whirl of the broncho pen.
The rush of the summer branding
When the work is rough and hard,
Beyond all understanding,
And the shivering nights on guard.
The quiet night in the summer
When the air is moist and warm;

You hear the rumbling thunder
And watch the approaching storm.
When the heavens pour like a funnel
And the Devil his own can claim;
When the sky is black as a tunnel,
Then white with the lightning's flame.
It is then that the weak go under;
It calls for a hardy breed.
The shattering crash of the thunder
And the rush of the mad stampede.
The terrible grip of the blizzard
When the horse and rider reel.
The curse of the snowblind puncher,
And the frost bites that throb and peel.
The nights you hate to remember
When you lay in the line camp alone
When the gray wolves howled in the timber
And the perishing cattle moaned.
You tried to prevent the slaughter,
But the frost and the storm were king.
How you chopped the ice from the water
And prayed for an early spring.
Or down in the desert regions
And the ranges far to the south.
Where the cattle swarm in legions
And the stock man is caught in the drouth.
Springs are steadily failing
Almost no place to go.
Coyotes are always wailing,
Buzzards are circling low.

What once were strong young cattle
Are only suffering wrecks,
So thin that they seem to rattle
When you stick your knife in their necks.
Cattle too weak to gather—
You must try it although you fail;
Holding them up in the "Prather"
"Chousing" them over the trail.
On every side they are crying,
"Take your cattle away;
Half of our own are dying—
No water and grass for strays."
Cowboys in clothing tattered,
Faces and hands brush scarred,
Saddles and chaps all battered,
Horses look gaunt and hard.
The heat and the dust that smothers,
The tired-out horse that lags,
The calves that have lost their mothers
Wailing along in the drags.

That's why I'm giving you warning—
There's something I cannot tell.
The joys as clear as the morning
The tortures akin to Hell.
They never will reach outsiders
Who were raised in the town's confines,
But they're here for the hard old riders
Who can read them between the lines.

—Bruce Kiskaddon, *Rhymes of the Ranges*

and recited by ranch people. They are still recited today.

Cowboy poetry is a continuing, constantly revitalized tradition. As the social and economic challenges facing ranching people grow, the writing of poetry seems to increase. Several hundred books and recordings of cowboy poetry are now available to the public, and each year nearly two hundred writing and reciting cowboys and ranchers, men and women, gather in Elko, Nevada, to share this poetic tradition at the Cowboy Poetry Gathering.

This event started in 1985 as the brainchild of folklorists in the West who were dissatisfied with stereotypes of the cowboy portraying him as laconic and non-expressive. The cowboy poetry tradition had been mostly a private one. To find cowboy poets we wrote letters to the editors of as many small western newspapers as we could find, asking for information about people who wrote cowboy poems or remembered traditional recitations. After hundreds of responses and thousands of miles of driving to remote ranches, we located nearly a hundred working or retired cowboys who either wrote poetry or recited older poems from the tradition. That first year we brought nearly fifty of them together in Elko, a small ranching town halfway between Salt Lake City and Reno. We were so uncertain about the consequences of making public what had been private for so long that we held the event in the middle of nowhere, in the middle of winter, reaching it by a train that got there in the middle of the night. I will never forget the feeling of that first gathering, when cowboys were finally given their own artistic forum. It was like uncorking an old and rare bottle of brandy. Within a week after this first event, the "Tonight Show" was calling for cowboy

Jon
Bowerman, Oregon cowboy,
performs his poetry at the Cowboy
Poetry Gathering, Elko, Nevada.

Cowboy poet
and singer Gary McMahan with his
yodeling dog at the Cowboy Poetry
Gathering, Elko, Nevada

poets. The headlines poured in: "Out Where the Sages Bloom, 120 Rhyme-Stoned Cowboys Show How the West Was Spun" came from *People*; "Poets, Lariats and Prairie Sages" and "Poem on the Range" appeared in *The Wall Street Journal*; and "Git Along Little Doggerels" topped a full page of coverage in *Newsweek*.

Since the first Cowboy Poetry Gathering, an extraordinary thing has happened: reciting poetry has become an accepted activity in rural areas of the West. Not only have several state and local gatherings sprung up, but one can find hundreds of performances of cowboy poets at local fairs, school programs, cattlemen's meetings, and the like. With this new popularity has come a kind of faddishness that has made some cowboys think that any words they jot down make a worthwhile poem and that has also produced a bunch of pretenders attempting to take advantage of the wave of interest. But despite this, cowboy poetry will remain a viable tradition in the West because at its heart it will be performed in the same places it has been for a hundred years: in the cowboy camp after a long day, at some bar when a memorized recitation can overcome a cowboy's shyness, or traveling, trying to stay awake on long rides between rodeos.

It must be obvious that the tradition of cowboy poetry paints pictures, tells stories, teaches lessons. But beyond poetry there is a vast network of informal allied traditions such as storytelling, joke-making, and tall tale-telling that are found wherever cattle and humans exist together. These informal oral traditions are accompanied by additional formalized literary traditions besides poetry. Cowboy essayists, writers of reminiscences, and journalists preserve ranching traditions through the written word. Writers like Frank King, who wrote a regular column for the *Western Livestock Journal*, are still fondly remembered by ranchers. Countless others have written regularly for small-town newspapers and regional cattlemen's publications over the years, including men such as Arnold Rejos, who wrote essays about the old ways of vaqueros and buckaroos.

Another ranching tradition is sketching, drawing, painting, and cartooning—what might be termed "visual narrative," because each work of art explores a situation or tells a tale. Like poetry, it is often subjective and impressionistic, yet to succeed with its audience it must contain the details of the cowboy's working life, must tell a pertinent story or teach a lesson, must be understandable yet thoughtful. Like cowboy poetry, visual art has a long history in the American West; most of the well-known cowboy artists have had a background in ranching. Many large crews have at least one cowboy who sketches as his contribution to the social life of the crew. This visual arts tradition was born of artists who may now be revered and copied, but who originally drew exclusively for a cowboy audience. A sketch was as ephemeral as a story, chalked on a canvas tent or traded for a drink.

Contemporary cowboys are particularly fond of the artwork of Charles Russell and of the novels and accompanying illustrations of Will James. These artists are well respected today, as cowboys often explain, because they "knew the life," because they shared their own respect for it through the care they took in portraying the details of the work. Little things like Russell's highly detailed gear, the set of the saddles, the look of the horses, all mean much more to cowboys than to art dealers.

Moorhouse
Ranch "tank," or pond, Benjamin,
Texas

This tradition of painting cowboys in the West has continued, but much of it is now changing to satisfy the demands of the lucrative Western art market, and it is now becoming increasingly peripheral to the lives and interests of cowboys and all but the most wealthy ranchers.

More central to the occupation are the cartoonists and illustrators whose work appears in the trade magazines of horsemen and cattlemen. Ranch cartooning is nearly as old a tradition as cowboy poetry, and for years ranching magazines have been carrying cartoons that are eagerly sought after and saved by ranching folks. One can't mention J. R. Williams's "Out Our Way" comics to the older generation without eyes lighting up. The same response is elicited from the present generation by mentioning Ace Reid and the characters in "Cowpokes." They are almost family. Hardly recognized by the formal art world and largely unfamiliar to the general public, they have a secure place in the West.

Of all the forms of cowboy art, cartoons are the most exclusive in their message. The usual style is to portray cowboys and animals in unbelievable situations. Often these cartoons make humorous comments on the same themes that cowboy poems

Oxbow Ranch horses, Prairie City, Oregon

During roping, a cow accidentally gets caught in the loop, creating a "wreck"; it takes seven cowboys to undo the rope, Moorhouse Ranch, Hall County, Texas

are likely to treat more seriously: the precariousness of cowboy work, the chanciness of ranch economics, or the odd kinds of social interaction in ranching communities. The stupidity of cows, tourists, and bureaucrats, and the foolishness of anyone who tries to bring people, horses, and cows

together in one place are frequent subjects. Yet the intent is not entirely satiric; Ace Reid's biographer John Erickson sums up Reid's success and the genre's appeal in this way: "His triumph as an artist/cartoonist/ storyteller is that he is able to depict frustration and suffering and helplessness

The old West
is still alive in southwestern
Wyoming.

Lone Colorado
cowboy waiting for the remainder of
the herd on a cold and windy
winter day

without self-pity and without stripping his characters of their dignity."

The wealth of folk expression—written and told, sketched and painted, braided and sewn—in a single, relatively uncommon occupation makes for theorizing. Why should cowboys have such a range of artistic forms readily available, established in conventional forms, and widely practiced? Does it have to do with the loneliness of the range, the respect for heritage, the deep-set individualism, the Hollywood myth? It is hard to know. The folklife of the cowboy includes working gear, costume, vocabulary, and speech styles, even the arrangements of the bunkhouse and line camp, the exact look of the pickup. Every cowboy, every rancher, every worker in the cattle industry makes personal statements about this occupation. Whether the statement be as formalized as a poem or illustration or as casual as a joke in passing or the choice of a feed cap rather than a cowboy hat, this is the folklore of the ranching occupation. The power of the life of the cowboy continues. Everyone who participates must contend with the power inherited. Some revel in it, others despair in it. But all hard riders know what it is to see between the lines.

Kim Smith, cow boss, working cattle on the open range at the Cottonwood Ranch, O'Neill Basin, Nevada

From CATTLE DRIVE, 1988

The drought was a bad one, as dry as a bone
That laid on the flats like alkali stone
It was hot and so dusty our color did change
And Sully, my buddy, was a strange shade of beige

• • •

But in spite of the heat and as well as the dust
We pulled and we pushed with a buckaroo's lust
Those fast old bovines morale seemed some low
'Cos the drought it took toll and made 'em real slow

We came down the road on that last and cold day
The ladies in front, breaking new trail
The trouble in Smith did not come again
They came through together, as if they were tame

Double
J. A. Land & Livestock cows moving
along a dusty road on the
Sweetwater Ranch, Bridgeport,
California

Now this year it's over, sad but so true
And a hell of a wait to come, buckaroo
But we'll be invited, again, I sure as heck know
'Cos Johnny's young heifers, each year, must go home

And at Bridgeport, November, we'll gather together
To ride on point, in the drag, whatever
We'll do what the captain of cattle explains
And try to do it without bitches and wails

Ascuaga, he tells us, he'll always have cattle
And on the way to Smith there'll always be battle
He needs us, he feeds us, he spoils and he hugs
But only because we're sleeping with bugs

But the truth is, old cowboys, we're veterans now
We know how to sleep, eat and drink, and we really know cow
We can cuss 'em and fuss 'em and ride all damn day
In sun, rain, and wind, or in blizzards that ache

But as soon as he calls and gives us the date
We'll hop in our four-bys and head for the gate
We'll trail that cattle as well as we can
Hoping, as usual, that John asks us back

—C. J. Hadley

MUSIC AND DANCE

GUY LOGSDON

He enjoyed riding and dancing better than anyone I ever knew, and over-indulgence in the two exercises caused an abscess to form on his liver which called him hence in 1876
—Branch Isabell,
The Trail Drivers of Texas

Riding and dancing are two activities common to all American cowboys. These cowboys come in all descriptions: tall and short, lean and fat, good-looking and ugly, sound in mind and body or broken in both, domesticated and wild, good dancers and bad dancers. Of course, I am referring to *working* cowboys, not urban cowboys, Nashville imitations, or Hollywood heroes. And these *working* cowboys call themselves punchers, buckaroos, cowpokes, vaqueros, or whatever term is common on their home range. No matter what description fits them or what they call themselves, most *working* cowboys enjoy riding and dancing. Very few can sing. In fact, they are more likely to recite a song along with other poems than they are to sing. They are no different today than their predecessors in the early trail-driving days.

The "singing cowboy" image is a part of the folklore that has grown with the Western myth; for, indeed, the American cowboy is the mythical hero of this nation. But the reality of working with cattle is dramatically different from the romantic image, particularly the singing cowboy image. The well-known song hunter, John A. Lomax, and other song collectors, dude-ranch balladeers, and Hollywood yodeling cowboys, along with phonograph records of Western crooners, created and perpetuate the singing cowboy image. Folklorists, historians, and song collectors have attempted to show that "cowboy songs" were work songs or, at least,

$\mathbf{S}$ettling
cattle to hold them while the
remainder of the herd catches up
requires patience and the ability to
move slowly, Double J. A. Land &
Livestock cattle drive,
California and Nevada.

riding songs. A few have written that the rhythm of each song falls within a particular gait—lope, walk, gallop, trot. However, a horse that has a stiffed-legged trot does not inspire a rider to break into joyful singing. Dallas Turner of Reno, Nevada, told me that the well-known and well-loved writer of cowboy songs and poems Curley Fletcher believed that for a song to be a "good" cowboy song, it had to be in three-quarter—waltz—time, and, indeed, many of the most popular "old" cowboy songs are in waltz rhythm. To sing such a song on horseback, a cowboy would have had to be riding a three-legged horse or a trained one, like Roy Rogers's Trigger.

Cowboy work is not romantic. Being kicked in the groin by a yearling, breathing dust all day, or freezing in rain and snow, being chased by a crazy-mad mother cow, or hooked by a horn, having a horse fall on you, breaking bones and popping-off fingers, doing dirty work, inhaling the odor of burning hair and flesh, and castrating bull calves do not inspire working cowboys to sing while they work. More likely, such things inspire them to create new curse words and other descriptive sayings that defy non-cowboy imagination. Only Hollywood and Nashville portray the always-clean, ever-fearless singing cowboy. The romantic image comes from the observer, not the participant.

Some cowboys did sing, but not work songs. During the trail-driving days, when trail herds were often massive in size, the night herders sang. They also whistled, played the fiddle, talked to themselves, and recited poems—anything to stay awake, break the monotony, and cover up fear. The human voice apparently could have a calming effect on some cattle—but the quality of most cowboy voices would have

started a stampede, not prevented one.

One writer has stated that cowboys racing at break-neck speed would sing out in an effort to turn or quell a stampede. That feat would require an amazing mind and a hell of a voice. Apparently, what is singing to some ears is yelling to others. Ramon Adams, an excellent historian of cowboy culture, quoted an old cowboy who said, "Them brutes don't have no ear for music." Certainly, I never heard a working cowboy with a smooth, clear voice. Instead, their voices sound as if too much sand and dust had settled in their throats.

There are working cowboys who still sing, and I have collected many songs from older cowboys, most of whom are now deceased. The songs vary in content, including songs about cowboys (commonly known as folk songs), bawdy songs, and sentimental songs from the nineteenth century. Each cowpuncher I collected from indicated that the songs were sung during leisure time and for recreational purposes, not as work songs.

The first-known collector of cowboy songs was N. Howard "Jack" Thorp, a horseman from New Mexico. In 1889 he started a song-collecting trek that led him into Texas, Indian Territory, and back to New Mexico. He published some of the songs in 1908 under the title, *Songs of the Cowboys* (Estancia, New Mexico), and he also wrote songs and poems. Thorp's best-known song is "Little Joe, the Wrangler," written in 1898.

John A. Lomax, who grew up as a Texas farm boy, heard cowboys sing and was captivated by the songs. He wrote down the words, and years later, in 1910, his collection was published under the title *Cowboy Songs and Other Frontier Ballads;* it quickly went into additional printings,

Dan Lufkin,
rancher, and Jake Williams, ranch
manager, share a contemplative
moment during the Oxbow Ranch
cattle drive, Prairie City, Oregon

and very few ranch houses were without a copy. The book became so popular that many songs became standardized according to the Lomax texts, so this book had a tremendous influence on the repertoire of singers of cowboy songs and on attitudes about cowboy singing. Lomax was a romanticist, but both he and Thorp did caution that many cowboy songs would singe the hair on a cow and were too vile to publish—Lomax obligingly laundered many songs in his collection.

"The Strawberry Roan" is the most widely known ballad among cowboys. Written in 1914 by the California-Nevada cowboy, Curley Fletcher, it spread throughout the West. Originally published as a poem, an unknown singer set it to music. A few years later, Fletcher wrote a humorous

bawdy version, "The Castration of the Strawberry Roan," which at least one scholar has deemed gross rather than humorous. Nevertheless, it is well known and enjoyed.

Other cowboy poets and songwriters contributed to the growing stockpile of cowboy songs—D. J. O'Malley, Charles Badger Clark, Jr., Gail Gardner, and many anonymous bards. John I. White, whose radio name in the 1920s and '30s was "The Lonesome Cowboy," has devoted much of his life to gathering information about specific cowboy songs and songwriters, publishing his work in 1975 as *Git Along, Little Dogies.* Also, Glenn Ohrlin, an Arkansas cowboy and rancher and a former rodeo cowboy, compiled his collection of songs and personal observations in *The Hell-Bound Train,* published in 1973. These two

Saddling up
the cowboy crew at the Sombrero
Ranch, Browns Park, Colorado

books, along with the Thorp and Lomax volumes, form the nucleus of a cowboy song collection, but they also indirectly perpetuate the false notion that cowboying automatically includes singing, a notion greatly influenced by Hollywood.

The success of Hollywood lies in its ability to capitalize on the romantic, gun-totin', individualistic cowboy image. The first successful film venture, "The Great Train Robbery," was a Western. The public loved the dime-novel cowboy as portrayed in films, and cowboy stars were created to fill the demand; most of them had to be taught how to ride a horse. William S. Hart had to learn, and even William Boyd (Hopalong Cassidy) and John Wayne. Both Boyd and Wayne maintained a lifelong fear of and dislike for horses.

There were genuine working cowboys who drifted into Hollywood, but they usually became stuntmen and extras. A few did become stars, most notably Ben Johnson. I know of no working cowboy who became a singing cowboy in Hollywood.

The singing cowboy was not ignored even in silent films. Scenes occasionally portrayed a cowboy or cowboys singing, of which the best example is seen in William S. Hart's classic *Tumbleweeds.* To indicate transitions in time and place he inserted scenes with three singing cowboys, sometimes in the saddle. Words on the screen let the audience sing along. Dancing was depicted even more often than singing in the early films.

The advent of sound was rough on some Hollywood cowboys, whose voices did not suit their rugged image. One exception was Ken Maynard, who made the transition to sound with great success, and with his background in Wild West and circus entertainment, he became the complete entertainer—an excellent rider, fiddle and guitar player, and singer.

Maynard was the movies' first full-time singing cowboy, but Hollywood specifically tailored "horse opry" movies for Gene Autry, "The Oklahoma Yodeling Cowboy" (actually, he had been a relief railroad telegrapher, not a cowboy). Autry's first film appearance was *In Old Santa Fe* (1934), in which Maynard starred. Autry's radio and recording success, coupled with the excellent reception his work in this movie received, inspired Republic Pictures to create a new type of film—the singing cowboy Western. The success of Autry's movies stimulated competition and the need for additional cowboy singers. The singing cowboys included Roy Rogers, Tex Ritter, Eddie Dean, Jimmy Wakely, and many lesser-known and seldom-remembered singers. Filmmakers even used "light opera" singers in their attempt to develop new "cowboy"

talent. Through the twenty years of singing cowboy films, the only star who carried much knowledge about real cowboy culture was Rex Allen, "The Arizona Cowboy."

In most horse opries, the star was backed up by an ensemble of singers, the best known of which was the Sons of the Pioneers, the group from which Roy Rogers came. The Sons established a close-harmony campfire image of group cowboy singing—a romanticized image beyond the wildest imaginings of any working cowboy. Their songs and singing were and continue to be popular throughout the West, and a dude ranch without a Sons-style sing-along group is a poor dude ranch indeed.

Millions and millions of movie fans and dude ranch visitors throughout the world think of Gene, Roy, or the Sons when cowboy music is mentioned; in reality, a recording of a genuine working cowboy singing would probably blow out the speakers of their sophisticated sound system. However, Red Steagall, George Strait, and

After-hours jam session, Cowboy Poetry Gathering, Elko, Nevada

Pageant at
Lambshead & Matthews Ranches,
Albany, Texas

Ian Tyson, whose roots are in the agriculture industry, represent the best combination of the real world, Hollywood, and Nashville. Glenn Ohrlin, Chris Le Doux, and Johnny Baker, who combine working cowboy and rodeo cowboy experience, are the best-known singers in the working cowboy tradition. Don Edwards also qualifies.

Nevertheless, there remains a vast chasm between the popular cowboy image and the real cowboy; for at the end of the day the cowboy does not relax by reaching for his guitar. In fact, the guitar is yet another element of the romantic image imposed on cowboys in the twentieth century. The fiddle was the instrument most often heard in cow camps, followed in popularity by the banjo, the four-string minstrel-show type. The fiddle was *the* musical instrument of the westward frontier movement. It was (and is) essential for a good dance, whether square, round, or ballroom. A dance band without a fiddler is not much of a dance band, and since many people considered dancing sinful, the fiddle was often called the "devil's box." When a fiddler "got religion," he often put it aside, never to play again. Of course, I don't know any cowboy fiddlers who have been confronted with that dilemma of choice.

In his classic narrative, *The Log of a Cowboy* (1903), Andy Adams tells of his family's removal to Texas after the Civil War and implies the essence of successful cowboying:

> By the time I was twenty there was no better cow-hand in the entire country. I could, besides, speak Spanish and play the fiddle, and thought nothing of riding thirty miles to a dance. The vagabond temperament of the range I easily assimilated.

Riding, dancing, and fiddling were Adams's formula for a happy cowboy life. Today, the cowboy drives his pickup to the dance, instead of going horseback or driving a buggy. The pickup is about the only major difference between past and present cowboying. The spirit of individuality and the ability to play as hard as they work have not changed. Descriptions of working cowboys in the post-Civil War era—formative years for the western cattle industry—also describe *some* of today's working cowboys.

In Texas or wherever the home range was, the cowboy exercised polite society behavior at dances, for the ranch-house dance was the common dance, and to attend it, cowboys and families traveled great distances. Ranch-house dances were held for a variety of reasons; any excuse to get

Don Edwards playing with a group of friends at the Cowboy Poetry Gathering, Elko, Nevada

people together, such days as the end of round-up, the Fourth of July, the eves of Thanksgiving, Christmas, and New Year, and any other day of celebration were always reasons to dance at a ranch house, school house, or other gathering place. Today, ranchers, county cattlemen's organizations, state organizations, and national organizations throw dances for the same reasons. When cowboys and their ladies get together, they dance.

The ranch-house dance was not always related to a particular event; sometimes it was held by someone who decided that it was time to get friends together again or to give newcomers a chance to get acquainted. Invitations traveled by word of mouth; rarely would written or printed announcements go out, for no one was to feel unwelcome through omission. "Everybody invited and nobody slighted."

Since long-distance travel was neces-

Cowboys in a ranch "rig" traveling along a Colorado highway

sary for many, early preparations were made to assure that everything was ready and that nothing would interfere with going to the dance. Buggies for cowboys were scarce and were usually rented from a livery stable in town. To have one to take a girl to the dance was desirable; one cowboy had a girl who lived

twelve miles from the ranch where he worked. To make arrangements with the girl, he rode twenty-four miles. To produce a buggy he rode sixteen miles to town and drove the same distance coming back, making thirty-two miles. Then he drove to

the girl's home, covering the twelve miles, and thence to the dance, covering eight miles. After the dance Bill drove the eight miles back to the girl's house, the twelve miles to the ranch, and made the thirty-two mile round trip to return the buggy. In all, Bill covered a distance of one hundred and twenty-eight miles, in order to take his "best girl" to the dance. (From "The Cowboy Dance" by John R. Craddock in *Publications of the Texas Folk-Lore Society, 2* [1923])

Nearby neighbors usually would stop

Sunset,
Prairie City, Oregon

A bottle of
a favorite brew on the fence of a
pen of bulls for sale at the Grand
National Livestock Exposition Range
Bull Sale, Cow Palace, San Francisco

by to help prepare; they would bring food or something to help the host provide meals and refreshments for the guests. Sundown was the common gathering time with enough of the early evening set aside for visiting. The fiddler or piano player and other musicians, if they were available, signaled the beginning of the dancing.

Food and drink were abundant; pride was taken in providing a good "feed." While coffee was the standard drink, whiskey was common, either in a barrel for all or in bottles hidden away where they could be easily found by those who wanted them. This practice depended on the attitude of the host and hostess; therefore, at a few dances, strong drink was difficult to find. Drunkenness was not acceptable behavior, though it was tolerated by letting the cowboy sleep it off somewhere out of the way. Rowdiness and fighting were taboo; anyone who committed such indiscretions departed for the evening. Such standards are still observed at these dances.

The ranch-house dance usually lasted all night long with individuals or couples leaving at a time that would allow returning to do morning chores before resting. The cowboy would announce that he was leaving and that the next dance was to be his last. The farewell dance was executed with a vigor that implied it truly might be his last. At some time, they knew, it *would* be his last dance.

Not all cowboys had the pleasure of attending the ranch-house dance or the town dance hall. They had to create their own dances. Around a campfire, in a bunk house, or in a saloon—all without women—wherever they were, they improvised. With enough whiskey in them and a great urge to dance, even a stag dance was a welcome pleasure. At the other dances, men supple-

mented the female dance partners; at the stag dance, it was complete substitution, and it can be assumed that the quality of characters at some of the stag dances might well have been those who were not welcome or at least had reason not to attend the ranch-house dances.

An old-time Arizona cowboy told me:

As I remember it, in my home settlement a bunch of young men—single men and teenage boys—would go to a school house, have a French harp. The ones which could play would take turns playing while the others danced. They didn't dance anything much but quadrilles. They would tie a handkerchief around the boy's arm or young men who were supposed to be the women or the girl. Then they would have a caller who would call off the dance changes which they were to go through. I don't see what kick they got out of it now, but they did it just the same. There weren't any bars or saloons to go to, except in Payson, and no females ever went near one of them at the time.

There were cowboys—few in number, at least among the bachelors—who, because of religious convictions, did not dance. Others

declined because they were sober, married men. Yet even these individuals attended the dances—standing along the wall. They *might* participate in "play-party" dances, which were not considered real dances and, therefore, were not sinful. Play-party activities were singing dances, without musicians or callers; skipping, marching, and dance movements were performed to the singing of the participants, who would swing one another by the hand instead of the waist. That made the play party acceptable to most churches, but less enjoyable for a cowboy. Modern-day square-dance clubs are an extension of the play-party morality.

The ranch dance, with its variations from couple dancing to play-party dancing,

has continued into the 1980s. The occasional traditional dance, one with *all* the elements, is still "thrown" from time to time. But the cowboy continues to dance in bars, saloons, and dance halls.

The twentieth century introduced many changes, and for the world of dance—even the cowboy's world of dance—the most important technological advancements were the phonograph and the radio. Dancers could dance without a fiddler, and the moral role of the play party was rendered ineffective, for now a couple could dance in private and pray in public. With recorded dances and calls, square-dance fans could organize for square dancing only. Such organizations began slowly to replace the

Barbeque
and dance held at the Lambshead & Matthews Ranches, Albany, Texas

Host Watt Matthews with Charles Schreiner III and Karol Combs during the "Sampler" barbeque and dance at the Lambshead & Matthews Ranches, Albany, Texas

play party in providing wholesome dance; no alcoholic beverages were allowed at the dance, and behavior had to conform to certain acceptable limitations. Square-dance clothing in the phonograph and radio age became a cross between country farmer and cowboy as they are conceived by city folks.

In western states that allow liquor by the drink, bars, not honky-tonks or road houses, are the popular watering-holes for cowboys. Beyond the Bible Belt influence of parts of Texas, Kansas, and Oklahoma, dancing with friends in a bar is not considered degrading, low-life, or sinful. In fact, many western bars have excellent dance floors and even live music, or at least a good juke box. *Families* can go into such a place and enjoy an evening of dancing.

In Texas, the ranch-house dance was combined with black blues and jazz and with a long, heavy bow fiddling technique to produce Western swing. The farm family of John Wills played many ranch dances in West Texas, and his oldest son, Bob, at an early age started fiddling at the dances with John. Steeped in the family tradition of fiddling, Bob went to Fort Worth in 1929, where he and a new friend, Herman Arnspiger, started playing "house dances"—similar to ranch dances. After a few years in Fort Worth as a member of radio's Light Crust Doughboys (the group was named after the flour mill that sponsored them), Bob organized his legendary Texas Playboys and found a home in Tulsa, Oklahoma.

In that town, on February 9, 1934, the Playboys went on the air for KVOO, and Cain's Ballroom became their dance headquarters. At first, they saw their radio program mainly as a vehicle for advertising dances. Soon, however, the broadcasts spread their fame far beyond Tulsa, and they made many recordings. Through the years, numerous dance bands grew out of the Wills organization, the best-known being Johnnie Lee Wills and His Boys, and Leon McAuliffe and His Cimarron Boys. In 1939 Bob sponsored a rodeo, the first Bob Wills Stampede in Tulsa; within four years it had become the Johnnie Lee Wills Stampede and continued as an annual event until the death of Johnnie Lee in 1984. But while the Wills were committed to pleasing the cowboys, Western swing also appealed to dancers throughout the West, cowboys or not.

Popular performers from cowboy culture who perpetuate the cowboy/Western swing tradition include Red Steagall, Ian Tyson, Reba McIntire, Pake McIntire, Pinto Bennett, and George Strait. Their success lies

Young square dancers during a talent competition at the Texas Ranch Roundup, Wichita Falls, Texas

in their ability to communicate with working cowboy dancers.

One other variation on the dance is found in the West—the small-town rodeo dance. When the population of a western hamlet is swelled by rodeo's competitive activity and festivity, fighting, drinking, *and* dancing increase—less on the part of the rodeo cowboys than the fans. Rodeo dances often resemble the end of the trail. Cowboys with broken legs can be seen hobbling around the dance floor with female partners; the promise and excitement of a close dance erase the pain of earlier battles.

At the smaller dances in cowboy country, each range has its favorite dances. In Oklahoma a "Paul Jones" mixer is danced at least three times in the evening; in Texas the "Cotton-Eyed Joe" is always in demand;

while in Arizona the old-timers call for "Put Your Little Foot," and the last dance of the evening is always "Home, Sweet Home." Cowboy dancing today differs from the past only in the inclusion of current dances; the traditional favorites are still favorites, maybe a polka or a patterned dance.

The cowboy dance is celebrated in cowboy songs and poems. Perhaps the most popular poem written about the subject is "The Cowboys' Christmas Ball" (1893) by Larry Chittenden. Others are Badger Clark's "Bunkhouse Orchestra," James Barton Adams's "At a Cowboy Dance," Robert V. Carr's "Bill Haller's Dance," Henry Herbert Knibbs's "The Cowboys' Ball," and many, many more, including "Big Cowboy Ball," "Did You Ever Do the Square?," and "The Old 'Square Dance' of the Western Range," which are reprinted in *The Trail Drives of Texas.* In country-western music, songs written and sung by such artists as Red Steagall about Bob Wills and cowboy dancing are heard with frequency. A popular Texas song about cowboy dancing in the modern tradition is "A Big Ball in Cowtown (We'll Dance Around)," always in demand throughout the Southwest. Contemporary cowboy poet Baxter Black has composed two songs about cowboy dancing in bars, "Midnight at the Oasis" and "Birds of Paradise."

From the poetry of the poet to that of the dance itself, and from the ranch house to the dance hall to the road house, the cowboy's love of dancing is a way of life. There is no reason to doubt the relationship of the cowboy to music and dance will endure.

Baxter and Cindy Lou Black join in with a group during the Cowboy Poetry Gathering, Elko, Nevada

NECESSITY AND FASHION

DICK SPENCER

The American cowboy is recognized the world over; yet he is an elusive rascal. One description does not fit them all. The cowboy is a conglomeration of *variables.* He can't be pinpointed, and he doesn't wear a *uniform.* Among the multitude of variables are the ranges he works on, the seasons he works, the job he is doing at the moment, and where he happens to be when you see him.

Working cowboys are found mostly on ranches, and right away this leads to many variations. Ranches can be big or small, modern or primitive, near town or remote, and vastly different in availability of grass, water, fencing, and such facilities as barns, sheds, corrals, and work pens. Ranches can be on the desert, or the plains, or in rolling hills, or in the mountains. Some ranch cowboys must contend with deep snow and blizzards, some must fight intense heat and drought. Some get it both ways! All must battle disease and insects.

Some ranches are owned outright, some are leased, and some are operated in conjunction with "government land," either federal or state. Some ranches are privately owned; some are owned by corporations. Some are cow-calf operations, some run only steers, and some raise only horses. I guess we'll have to mention sheep ranches, too, but right now we're just talkin' cowboy.

Some ranches hold onto the old ways, some employ all the new developments available. There are still bunkhouses, cow-camps, line shacks, and chuck wagons—

 Wet cowboy boots hanging to dry on a fence post after a day's cattle work in the rain, Hall County, Texas

but not on all ranches.

The Longhorn, Hereford, and Angus cattle are still around, along with some older breeds, but the "exotic breeds" and crossbreds have invaded cow country in recent years. Some cowboys can't pronounce the name of the cattle they are trailing, but a cow is a cow, and cowboys work with cows!

So hunker down and let's discuss cowboy *wear* and *gear*, or what the cowboy wears and the gear he uses to do the job he does.

First off, everything is functional, for both the cowboy and his horse. Once the functional part is taken care of, the decoration starts. Cowboys take great pride in their equipment, readily admitting that once it's right then it can be prettied up. Cowboy gear is usually prettied up with stamping,

tooling, carving, engraving, braiding, stitching, lacing, or with the addition of brass, copper, silver, or even a touch of gold.

A cowboy's gear reflects his ability, pride, and personality, so he wants it to look good; but it is still *working gear*, so he stops far short of the glitter of the parade saddle group or the Western entertainer.

Fashion plays a big part in Western wear and gear, and it is most closely adhered to in the rodeo and horse-show world. A world champion cowboy can help set fashions, and so can successful horse-show riders and trainers. The rodeo and show circuit has added much to the color and style of Western wear. Over the years, working cowboys have added much as well, but at a slower rate. Instead of just rust and baling wire, the early Californios added beauty with silver and engraving, which we have already mentioned. Cowboys in other areas scoffed at first, then slowly imitated the style, as they took more and more pride in the tools of their trade. One example can be found in the beautiful Santa Barbara cheeks on bits. Originally designed for the spade or halfbreed bits of that area, Santa Barbara cheek designs can now be found on a wide variety of other mouthpieces where spades and halfbreeds are not used.

All the "fancy" hasn't been added in recent years, either. Any collector of cowboy gear can show and tell with his collection of old-time treasures. He has chaps, wristcuffs, bridles, and so on decorated with brass or nickel spots in various designs, brands, or initials, and bits and spurs decorated with silver, brass, and copper. Most of this is executed in designs the cowboy understands, like hearts, diamonds, clubs, and spades, or longhorns, acorns, flowers, and stars. His bits and spurs might be in the shape of gal or lady legs, pistols, goose

Saddles in for repairs, J. M. Capriola, Elko, Nevada

Saddle
blanket airing out on top of saddle;
during a lunch break horses are
often unsaddled and allowed to rest
and graze.

Fern Sawyer, rancher, showing off some of her colorful wardrobe, Nogal, New Mexico

necks, eagle beaks, or rattlesnakes. Yep, the old-timer had an eye for style, too!

It's still around today, with an even wider set of choices. The old look is still around and accepted by young cowhands and blends in well with the new look. The expression "clothes make the man" is not true of cowboys, however. Top hands can wear just about anything they like—a top hand being one who is doing the right thing in the right place at the right time. Their preferences are designed by necessity, and they create their own fashion by personal taste and vanity.

Spending several thousands of dollars in a good Western store isn't going to make a man a cowboy. Cowboys can usually tell "if there's a cowboy inside them clothes" by looking a man over. If there is a doubt, most will reserve their opinion until they see him work. Like the song says, "Don't Call Him a Cowboy, Until You've Seen Him Ride." There's another old song, too, that

sticks in the back of their minds, about a "Cowboy in a Continental Suit!"

Cowboys fall into many different categories, like stockyard, feedlot, rodeo, little outfit, big outfit, weekend, or whatever. All of them qualify for the title of cowboy, but for a moment we'll just split them into two groups: cowboys and buckaroos.

To make things easy, let's say the cowboy originated in Texas and the buckaroo started in California. The Texas cowboy spread far and wide, most especially after the Civil War. Texas was full of beef-on-the-hoof, and a hungry nation needed beef back east. Cattle drives were established over several trails up from Texas to the railroads in Kansas. Then, later, they moved herds to help stock new ranges in New Mexico, Colorado, Wyoming, Montana, and other areas.

The buckaroo actually predates the cowboy, because he came to California in the mission era, from about 1769 to 1823. The very word *buckaroo* comes from the Mexican word *vaquero*, "one who works with cows." Like the cowboy, the buckaroo moved north—to Nevada, Oregon, and Idaho—and seeped into Washington, Montana, and Wyoming. Some big outfits showed a blend of both the cowboy and the buckaroo. They did the same job, working with cattle, but they dressed differently and used different gear and methods. Nobody really cared, as long as they got the job done.

The primary job of the cowboy today is the same as it always was—to turn grass into beef. Of course, nowadays there is another step, the feedlot, where beef goes before going to the packing plant.

To simplify the differences between the cowboy and the buckaroo, let's start with appearance. Hats are blocked differently, both the crown and the brim. North-

Hat blocks at
Tom Hirt's Weather Hat Shop,
Penrose, Colorado

ern hat blocks are designed to shed rain, southern hat blocks will hold water. The southern cowboy usually punches the block out of his hat when it *does* rain, and snaps it back in when the rain quits, and thus his hat is cleaned.

All these blocks and creases have names, and even these vary by locale. Some are named after people, or places, or the way they look; like the Tom Mix crease, the Ft. Worth crease, the beaver slide, or the Pikes Peak crease, and even non-cowboys know what the pork-pie crease looks like. Some of the old creases have stayed the same, with the name changing to suit modern times. The old Wyoming crease (that looks like the cavalry campaign hat of the 1920s, pinched together at the top with four dents) went through a period as the Smokey-the-Bear crease and has recently been updated to the Phillips screwdriver crease.

The brim of the hat is different. The buckaroo likes a flat brim or snapped down in front. The cowboy's hat brim is usually curled up on both sides, with a sort of a point in front. The buckaroo might wear a stampede string under his chin; a cowboy scoffs at this. There are jokes, too, that go along with this. "Cowboys curl the sides of their hats up so's they can ride three in a pickup!" or "Buckaroos wear stampede strings because if their hat blows off, they can't git back on their horses if they git off!"

The "reservation" or "Injun block" got its name because Indian cowboys wore their hats just like they came out of the box, no crease and a flat brim. With the advent of television and the "Bonanza" series, the tall-crowned hat with no block in it got renamed the "Hoss" because of the character played by Dan Blocker. The narrower-brimmed western hat was called the *stockman*, or the *rancher* hat; and when it got curled,

sweat through, and dirtied up, it was called the *brush-popper.* Not all cowboys are brush-poppers, but all brush-poppers are cowboys. Wide-brimmed hats don't work well in heavy brush country.

When cowboys put their hats down, they place them upside down, on the crown, so they won't spoil the under-brim curl. Many of the northern blocks have to be hung on a nail, peg, hat rack, or set of antlers because they won't stand upside down on their crowns.

For the old-time cowboy, the red or blue cotton bandana was his neckwear, washcloth, towel, hot pad, and tourniquet. To put it on, he triangled it and put it on over his nose and tied it in back, like a holdup man. Then he pulled it down, over his shirt front. When he "rode drag" or worked in the dust, he could pull it up over his nose again to keep from breathing dust all day.

The buckaroo wears a *wild rag,* often of silk. It is considerably larger than a bandana and is also triangled with the point down in front and the ends wrapped around the neck and tied with a square knot in front. It serves primarily to ward off the cold. Both, of course, can be used for interchangeable purposes, and silk was not unknown to cowboys in the Southwest.

The cowboy as well as the buckaroo both liked vests and still do. "Never enough pockets to go around." The old-timer used the vest to carry his tally book, a pencil stub, a pocket watch (with a fancy fob or chain, or a leather thong), and the makin's for a Bull Durham smoke.

In the old days the cowboy wore any kind of work shirt, chambray being popular in warm weather and Pendleton woolens in cold. Both are still around. Today, a "Western shirt" automatically means a shirt with two pockets, special wrist cuffs, and a front and back yoke worked into the pattern. Snap fasteners for buttons on the front, wrists, and pockets add the final touches. The snap fastener button is a great invention, but it came too late for the early-day cowboys. Back then, shirts came in small, medium, and large sizes, and each size had only one sleeve length. Tall cowboys had lots of wrist showing, and short fellers had to wear garters to hold their sleeves up.

During this era leather wristcuffs and gauntlet gloves became popular. The cowboy claimed the wristcuffs "kept him from wipin' his nose on his sleeve." The truth was that, in brush country, it kept branches from getting in the slit in the forearm of the shirt and tearing it. When buttons were torn off, the cowboy had a problem. The snap fastener sure would have been welcomed by the old-timer! The first form-fit cowboy shirts didn't allow room for a wristwatch. Today, the wristwatch has almost replaced the old pocket watch.

Not too long ago down clothing entered the Western world of fashion and won immediate acceptance. It is warm, lightweight, and colorful. Down vests and jackets are great for the horseback rider, being warmer but lighter and less bulky than most of the old cold-weather gear. Down clothing gets its name from its goose-down filling, of course, but some of it is filled with wonderful man-made insulation fibers.

You can write a whole book just on saddles, but we'll settle for a quick look-see. There have been many changes over the years, and some of the old styles are returning. A rider has plenty of opportunity to select a working saddle to suit his own tastes and to help him in the job he does.

There are saddles for range work, arena work, cutting, roping, pleasure, or anything else a man has to do on horseback; and they can be as plain or as fancy as he desires or can afford.

When a rider buys a saddle, he has many choices. Stirrups, for instance, come in many styles, sizes, and shapes—anything from the narrow and rounded oxbow to the deep and wide calf roper's stirrup. Originally, the cowboy's stirrup was just a wide wooden "doghouse" style. Later stirrups were covered with brass and made in different shapes. Then some were covered with rawhide or leather, laced on, and then came a period when iron stirrups were fashionable. These came in a number of styles and shapes.

The iron stirrup wouldn't crush your foot in it if a horse fell, but it *could* break a horse's ribs. Then another problem surfaced. If a horse blew up with you as you were mounting, it sure wasn't any fun having an iron stirrup popping and waving in front of you, at about the level of your teeth. So iron stirrups faded out of style.

In recent years, however, they have emerged again, dressed up with some silver ornamentation on the outside. Aluminum, brass, and bronze stirrups have appeared; and steady inroads have been made by Ralide, a super-tough polymer.

Taps, from the Mexican word *tapaderos*, can be an addition to the stirrup, too. On kids' saddles they are called hoods, as they were also called in the old U.S. Cavalry. The primary purpose of taps was to keep the foot from slipping all the way through the stirrup, preventing the rider from getting "hung up and dragged," always a very real dread of cowboys riding alone in rugged range country. Taps also help protect the rider from cactus, brush, protruding dead

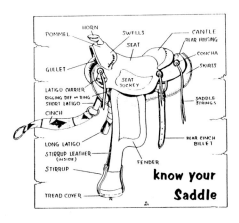

know your Saddle

A double-rigged stock saddle. The front cinch is affixed to the short latigo, pulled under the horse and tightened with the long latigo. The rear cinch is kept on the off (right) rear billet, pulled under the horse and tightened with the near (left) billet.

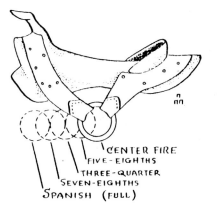

CENTER FIRE
FIVE-EIGHTHS
THREE-QUARTER
SEVEN-EIGHTHS
SPANISH (FULL)

Positions for front rigging on a saddle. Double-rigged saddles have the rear rigging ring just below where the cantle joins the saddle seat. A center-fired rig is always a single-rigged saddle.

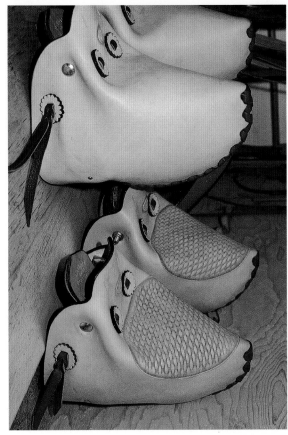

J. M. Capriola
craftsman making stirrups, Elko,
Nevada

Hand-crafted
covered stirrups, called tapaderos,
J. M. Capriolas, Elko, Nevada

branches, and even from foul weather. They come in different styles and shapes; from raw, green hide with the hair on, to such styles as bulldog, monkey nose, or eagle beak. Some have flaps that hang low enough to sweep the tops of sagebrush as you ride. They are functional but can also be decorated with stamping, tooling, or conchas.

Even saddle horns come in a wide range of designs for special jobs, such as cutting, barrel racing, and dally roping. Old-time bronc saddles had horns on them, but in recent years professional rodeo bronc riders have eliminated them from their Association saddles. The Association saddle, as you might guess, is built to strict specifications especially for rodeo contestants.

Ropes have been called by many names:

catch-rope, throw-rope, riata, lariat, gut-line, maguey, manila, nylon, lass-rope, but are almost *never* called a lasso by ropers. They are made of manila (hemp), maguey (a cactus fiber), braided rawhide, nylon, and even some of the newer poly fibers.

The old-time Texan was a hard-and-fast man, meaning his rope was tied to the saddle horn. If you rope something this way, either you got *it*, or it's got *you*. The dally man ropes something, then takes turns around the saddle horn with the rope to hold onto it. The word *dally* comes from the Mexican expression *da le vuelta*, meaning "give the turn" around the horn, when you've caught something.

Dally roping has made big inroads on all roping on the open range. When you're

Nylon
catch rope, or lariat, a standard
cowboy tool, attached to a saddle in
California

Stirrups
hanging for sale, J. M. Capriola

Rope tied
hard and fast around the horn

Braided horn
knot for hard-and-fast roping

headed for a wreck, you can "give the critter the rope instead of the ranch." This, of course, means "let him go before you get killed!" Cowboys carry ropes just over thirty feet long and wrap innertube rubber around the horn to hold their dallies. Buckaroos carry at least double that length of rope, and put mule hide around the saddle horn, so their dallies will slip and give a little.

Cowboys wear chaps (pronounced *shaps*, not like chapped lips), and these come in several styles: batwings, shotguns, or woolies (angora or bear). Some Texans still call chaps *leggins*. Buckaroos usually wear chinks, short chaps that come just below the knee. Cowboys traditionally made fun of the buckaroo and his shorty chaps, but these days chinks can be seen from South Texas to Canada. They are lighter in weight, make it easier for the rider to get on and off his horse, and they are a lot less trouble when working on the ground at brandings: "nobody standin' on your batwings when you try to get up!"

Even today, chaps and chinks can get fancied up as much as the wearer wants,

Moorhouse
Ranch cowboys braiding the horn knot to rope hard and fast, Hall County, Texas

Kim Smith,
cow boss, Cottonwood Ranch, dally
roping while branding calves, O'Neill
Basin, Nevada

Truet Self,
"The Hackamore Man," with
hackamores he hand crafted of
nylon rope, rawhide, and leather. A
hackamore is a bridle that requires
no bit.
opposite, top

Horsehair
hitched "mecaté"—also called a
"McCarte" or "McCarthy"—Big Loop
Rodeo, Jordan Valley, Oregon
opposite, bottom

with conchas, fringe, contrasting leather colors, buckstitching, and whatever else suits his taste. For the most part, buckaroo gear accents beauty more than cowboy gear does—more silver, tooling, engraving, and braided rawhide, reflecting the old Spanish and Mexican practice of first making it *useful*, then making it *beautiful*. The Santa Barbara cheeks (sides of the bit, outside the horse's mouth) on buckaroo spade bits are truly "horse jewelry." Rein chains help the balance on braided rawhide reins and protect the rawhide from water when a horse drinks with the bit in his mouth. Braided buttons on the reins and romal are for both balance and beauty. (The romal is basically a quirt attached to the reins.) Buckaroos also like horsehair or mohair McCarties (from the Mexican *mecate*, rope) with fancied-up snaffle bits and with "slobber leathers" to protect the reins when the horses drink.

The Texas cowboy rode a full double-rigged saddle; the buckaroo rode a California center-fire single rig (one cinch). Saddles are rigged in different positions, such as full, seven-eighths, three-quarters, or center-fire. The center-fire is a single rig, the others almost always double-rigged (two cinches). A pleasure rider can get by with a three-quarter single if he doesn't rope and stays out of rough country.

In the early days all cowboy saddles had high cantles and slick forks. Later, swells were added to the fork (front part of the saddle). The cowboy adopted this to help him stay aboard a horse that might "pitch" in Texas or "buck" anyplace else. Some of these swell-forks got so big and outlandish they became known as *bear-traps*. They would hold you in, even when you wanted out.

The buckaroo stayed with the slick-fork saddle, but added bucking rolls. These are horsehair-stuffed leather projections that fasten to the saddle on each side behind the horn, and they help a rider stay aboard a bucking horse. The buckaroo also stayed with his center-fire saddle for a long time, but in recent years a noticeable swing has been made to a three-quarter double rig.

Years ago you could tell about where a cowboy or buckaroo came from by his gear. But times have changed. It started with mail-order catalogs sent from big western stores located in cities that had magical names in the West—names like Fort Worth, Denver, and Cheyenne. Then came other names like Pendleton, Elko, and Visalia, and the number grew steadily. These catalogs became "cowboy wish books," and working hands could see what other cowboys were wearing and using in other parts of cow country. The blending speeded up.

Horse transportation got easier with horse trailers, stock trailers, and stout pickup trucks. Stockmen traveled greater distances to major stock shows and rodeos, and the blending continued. Saddle shops turned into "Western stores," and Western stores cropped up in more and more places, with a wide variety of Western wear and gear. Horse magazines played a part, too, with national advertisers showing what was available to all.

Most of the big-name saddlemakers from the turn of the century are no longer around. Names like Frazier, Flynn, Gallup, Mueller, Myres, Miles City, Meanea, Coggshall, Porter, Hamley, and a host of others are all gone, history now. The saddles they produced can still be found in ranch country; some are still used, some stored away, and many are in the hands of collectors.

The same is true of spur and bit makers, saddle-tree makers, and other famous manufacturers. The products are still available, of course, with talented individuals still producing some of the finest gear to be found.

Individuality remains a key word among cowboys and buckaroos. They don't have a uniform or a dress code, and you don't go into a Western store and "buy a cowboy suit." Cowboys from the same ranch can buy from the same store, and they will still retain their individuality. They don't all

Checking the
fit of a saddle at the J. M. Capriola
trailer display during the Big Loop
Rodeo, Jordon Valley, Oregon

Texas cowboy
wearing chinks and high-top boots
with oxbow stirrups

look alike, but they'll all look like cowboys.

Even the "cowboy belt" has room for variety in taste. To most people, a cowboy belt has a big buckle, some fancy tooling, and the wearer's name or nickname stamped on the back. This was not always so. Suspenders, or galluses, were frequently worn by the old-timers and are enjoying a return to popularity in some areas today. Back in the 1920s and 1930s, the ranger belt was common in Texas. It overlapped, had a neat fancy buckle with a couple of keepers and a tip. Ranger belts are still around; but, then as now, some old cowboys still don't wear any belt while they are working. One short-lived rodeo belt was the "bronco belt." It was six or eight inches wide in back, had two or three small buckles in front, and looked more like a motorcycle belt than something a cowboy would wear.

The big buckle actually came in because of the rodeo cowboy with his trophy buckle.

This buckle is still around today and is the most readily recognizable cowboy belt. Not only that, but the buckles are getting bigger and fancier, and the belts are tooled, colored, and adorned with buckstitching. Some have cutouts, with underlying colored leather, and some have silver-lettered names on the back instead of names just stamped on.

Belts and hatbands reflect the individual wearer's taste and flair, which cowboys have in abundance. Braided horsehair and hitched horsehair are common. Some cowboys make their own, and some buy them. A lot of excellent horsehair products used to be made in penitentiaries including bridles, McCarties, belts, and hatbands. They took time to make, and that's something convicts had plenty of. In fact, on a smaller scale, some prison inmates are still making those items.

In snake country, lots of snake skins end up on the cantles of saddles, around oxbow stirrups, or decorating belts or hatbands. A fresh-skinned rattler has a natural glue on the inside of his hide, and this sticks readily to a cantle-binding or a stirrup. More than one young puncher with his saddle so decorated has started to pick up his saddle, spotted the "rattler," and jumped back—only to look around quickly to see if anyone saw him do it.

Hatbands and belts have also been decorated with small conchas, nickel or brass spots, Indian beadwork, and whatever seemed right at the time. Just a few years back it was bird feathers strung on a band. They got so common they went out of favor in a hurry. No cowboy wants a "road kill" on his hat!

The cowboy boot has gone through a lot of transition to arrive where it is today. In the early days of the trail drives, following the Civil War, it hadn't evolved into the distinctive shape it now has. In fact, in these early times a pair of boots didn't have a left and a right; you just bought a pair of boots and wore them on the same feet until they made their own left and right by shaping themselves. It's no wonder the old-time cowboy didn't like to walk! One other interesting note: any bootmaker who has been in business for a long time can tell you that the average size of the cowboy boot has grown considerably in recent years. Many of the old-timers liked small, tight-fitting boots. Today's cowboys like a little more room for their feet. Not many things seem worse than putting on tight boots over wet socks when you crawl out of a bedroll before daylight. And when you *do* get them on, your toes are folded back under your foot until about noon.

Cowboy boots today come in various heights, a wide selection of scallops (the notches cut down the front and back),

varying rows of stitching, and a wide selection of leathers, colors, toes, and heels. No matter what you come up with, it's still a cowboy boot and it is recognized, admired, and worn the world over.

You can still buy boots with inlays or overlays, and personalized with brands, initials, or any distinctive ornamentation you might think up. The rows of fancy stitching evolved about as much for necessity as for beauty. The light, soft leather on some of the boot tops had to be reinforced with stitching to keep the leather from wrinkling and sagging down around the ankles, so the number of rows of stitching affects the durability, the beauty—and the price!

The original cowboy boot was designed for comfort and protection. It had a moderately pointed toe to help "find a stirrup"

Rattlesnake skin stretched across the cantle of a saddle

and a high, undershot heel to help you hold a stirrup. The high heel was "easy to set on," because a cowboy at work in a corral didn't have much time to sit down. When he had a chance, he would "hunker down," or sit on his heels. In the early days of bulldogging, the high, undershot heels could help a rodeo hand slide until the steer stopped, but today a "'doggin' heel" is just the opposite. It is a low heel, so a big hunk of a cowboy can dig in and stop-an'-flop his steer quicker. Most 'doggin's are won in less than five seconds, and the old-timers used to *slide* longer than that!

One cowboy boot doesn't quite fit the mold, but it is now recognized as a sure-nuf cowboy boot. It is called the roper's Wellington. Some calf ropers discovered that the British Wellington boot was light and easy to run in, so they adopted it. They added a scallop to "give it that cowboy look," and now it comes in all colors and is popular with both men and women.

Some cowboys wear their pants inside their boots, some wear them outside. Either way is acceptable, and neither of 'em is going to make you a cowboy if you ain't.

Spurs have long been accepted as the symbol of the riding man, and cowboys and buckaroos are proud that they are of that clan. Spurs run the full gamut of choices, from the plain to the fancy. Usually made of iron or stainless steel, they can be decorated with overlay and inlay in silver and gold, and ornamented with engraving. They may have narrow or wide heel bands, long or short shanks that curve up, straight back, or down, and rowels that range from small to large and from blunt to sharp. Rodeo cowboys have offset shanks (turned in at varying degrees) for riding broncs or bulls. Some spurs have chain or leather straps going under the boot instep to keep them from climbing up the boot, others do not. Rodeo bronc and bull riders sometimes use tie-downs and tie-ups on their spur shanks to hold them snugly in place. The loose hide on a Brahma bull is hard to hold onto with a spur that wobbles up and down, and it sometimes ends up being a two-thousand-pound bootjack!

Jinglebobs (small metal drops) were sometimes added outside the rowels to make "spur music" for the rider. They made a pleasant bell-like sound as he jogged along on his horse, and sounded good when a cowboy walked. Jinglebobs almost died out, but a few die-hard buckaroos and cowboys kept on wearing them, and they are now being seen (and heard) again in rapidly increasing numbers. Crusty old hands won't admit it, but I've watched 'em stick their heels into sage or brush as they ride, just to hear the rowel buzz and the jinglebobs sing.

Raised in Jordon Valley's buckaroo country, my wife always wears jinglebobs. Once, after a nine-day pack trip in Yellowstone, I got a phone call from a Montana cowboy who asked, "Were you and Viv on a pack trip in Yellowstone last week?" I told him we were, and he said, "We saw you pass on the trail, and I saw Viv's turquoise chinks and heard her jinglebobs, so I knew it was you folks! My wife wouldn't believe me, so I'm callin' to win our bet."

Even spur straps come in many shapes and sizes, varying from plain to fancy. Some are designed to be buckled inside, others outside, and some rodeo contestants like them buckled on top of the instep. Some old patterns had no buckles at all, just slots cut in the leather that could be pushed over the spur buttons on the side of the spur. Even today, spurs buckled to hang low and loose are said to be "in the town notch,"

because they sounded good when the old-time cowboy walked on the board sidewalks in town. So feel free to buckle your spurs inside or outside, but be sure you aren't wearing them upside down. When spurs have "chap guards" on the shanks, the chap guard is on the top side of the shank.

Two brand names heavily implanted in Western lore are still around, Stetson and Levi's. At one time all cowboy hats were called Stetsons, and all cowboy jeans were called Levi's. John B. Stetson made his first "big hat" in Colorado, during the 1859 gold rush there, and sold it for five dollars in gold, mined in Cripple Creek on the west face of Pikes Peak. Levi Strauss made his first pair of britches for a miner about ten years earlier during the California gold rush of '49. The denim sailcloth made the pants tough, and the copper rivets kept the pockets from tearing when the miner carried ore samples in them. The word *denim* comes from *cloth de Nîmes*, the durable sailcloth that was made in Nîmes, France. Old Levi Strauss had a large supply of this on hand, never suspecting he would start a fashion trend that would cover the world.

Stetson and *Levi's* became synonymous with *cowboy hat* and *cowboy pants*, and later other brand names popped up and became popular, too—once they had earned the respect of cowboys. Today there are many well-regarded brands making big hats and cowboy denims.

A couple of other innovations popular today are the baseball cap and the satin jacket. Like 'em or not, the baseball cap is here, and cowboys *do* wear them: mostly on windy days, or at jackpot ropings, or driving to the feed store in a pickup. But not in rodeo arenas! Cowboys don't have baseball team names on their caps—usually it's advertising names for just about anything agricultural, from tractors to rodeos to snuff or feed stores and on down the line. The satin jackets also carry logos of all kinds, including rodeos, riding clubs, outfitters, high schools and colleges, and even *Western Horseman* magazine. They are light, bright, colorful, and can ward off a chill wind.

Fashion is often fickle, and the "old" keeps cropping up and coming back again, even in things Western. Many manufacturers are now remaking old-time saddles, bridles, wristcuffs, bits, spurs, and so on. Restoring old gear has become a big business, even extending to wagons, buggies, harnesses, and the like; because of severe winters and rising gasoline prices, many ranchers are returning to horse-drawn bobsleds for winter cattle feeding.

The old cowboy's "fish slicker" has almost disappeared from the scene. It was made back East, as foul-weather gear for fishermen, but was redesigned for the working cowboy. It was yellow, came almost to the ground, and was slit up the back so you could straddle a horse; a special flap covered the saddle cantle and anything you might have tied behind. Although they were called pommel slickers, these garments almost always were tied behind the cantle when they were not being worn. Fresh oil had to be applied to it every now and then, because when it was tied behind the cantle, the saddle strings would crack the material slightly and cause it to leak.

My old yellow fish slicker is now tied behind a turn-of-the-century saddle in our Colorado Springs Pioneer Museum. When it finally leaked like a sieve, I used it to sack out colts for a few years, then I gave it to the museum. Just about everybody else had thrown theirs away.

Yellow slickers are still tied behind cantles all over cow country, but they are now made out of different materials that don't require coating with fish oil. The Aussie "outback" or "Snowy River" oiled slicker has caught on in recent years, especially in mountain country, because it is both warm and dry.

Another recent returnee from the old days is the duster. Most people remember them from paintings of nineteenth-century stagecoach robbers, and now they are back in fashion. Actually, they weren't cowboy gear in the old days; they were designed for men riding the stage, wagons, buggies, or horseback. They were made to keep dust off of the wearer's good clothes. When a feller got to town he could take off his duster and be dressed in his best go-to-meetin' clothes. Today, they *are* considered

Horse
halters hanging on a corral

cowboy gear, and some will even shed rain, though most are simply dust protectors and will just strain the rain when it falls—so only the little-bitty drops get to you.

Not too many years ago you could see horses in a halter class wearing plain old Johnson rope halters. Today, most halter horses wear leather halters covered with engraved silver that costs more than the horse and saddle I used to ride. Not only that, but exhibitors in the show ring are dressed in Western coordinates that make them look better than *we* did at weddings and funerals.

Styles and fashions come and go, but one thing is certain. A cowboy still looks like a cowboy. He still works outdoors, in the saddle, and in all kinds of weather on all kinds of terrain. You can bet he'll be wearing and using the clothes and gear that get the job done. And these will continue to reflect his pride in being a cowboy or buckaroo.

A PERSONAL POSTSCRIPT

As for me, I have had the opportunity to travel the West extensively, and much of it horseback. I was raised in Texas but have ranged far afield. I dress primarily to cover my nekkidness and just to look like me. I still buckle my spurs inside, and I like wagon-wheel rowels, tall red-top boots with high undershot heels, black hats, red shirts, and good-fitting jeans stuffed inside my boots. And I like leather vests.

I've got all kinds of chaps and chinks, and I prefer chinks for most riding—except in bitter cold or through heavy brush. I like a dally horn on a three-quarter double-rigged saddle, with a fairly high cantle and a rawhide binding, and I like saddle strings on my saddle. I like a thirty-two-foot, $\frac{7}{16}$-inch nylon rope, either true or scant, and I like it better after it's been used enough to fuzz out a bit. I like rubber around my saddle horn.

I've got my own preferences on how I like to gather cattle, move cattle, and work cattle. At brandings, I have preferences on the way things should be done—though wherever I go, I "do it their way." I have been most fortunate to have been on some of the big outfits as well as some of the smallest. I've been on some of the best run and some of the worst; but everywhere I went I was able to learn *something*. I've probably reached the age where I won't be changing my ways or my gear too much in the future. I'll probably stay Dick Spencer until I'm hauled off to the taxidermist.

So let me add one more line about Western wear. That's what I wear. Even when traveling abroad. I don't really care what anyone thinks of what I wear, even if it might look out of place in Paris, Rome, London, or Tokyo. I'd much rather they'd see me as I am than have one of my friends see me in a little dinky hat and shoes with laces. *That* I would never live down.

When I see another big hat in any airport in the world, I know we'll have something to say to each other, maybe we even have mutual friends, or have been to the same events, or have ridden the same trails.

RODEO

RANDY WITTE

Rodeo is the cowboy sport, born of the cattle industry, built on a bet—the "cowboy who couldn't be throwed" matched with "the horse that couldn't be rode." Today, rodeo is a multimillion-dollar business involving horses and cattle, competition and entertainment. Rodeo is an annual community event; county fairs, particularly in the West, offer it as part of the three- or four-day celebrations of agriculture and the fruits of harvest. Rodeo is part of the big indoor livestock shows.

There's a show-business side of rodeo—the grand entry, clown acts, trick riding and roping, trained animal acts—that dates back to 1882, when Col. William F. "Buffalo Bill" Cody got the idea of staging a Western extravaganza in the town of North Platte, Nebraska. At least one account of that show says there was a herd of buffalo, some Indians, and a stagecoach on hand. Col. Cody put Buffalo Bill's Wild West Show on the road and headed for the eastern crowds. It's harder to say what constituted the first rodeo itself, but the North Platte rodeo is still held each year in June and claims to be the first organized one in existence. Other rodeos, notably those in Pecos, Texas, and Prescott, Arizona, make similar claims, and the little prairie town of Deer Trail, Colorado, east of Denver, is reported to have been the site of a bronc-riding contest some time back in the late 1800s.

Rodeo is a life-style for many families. Children are raised in youth, high school, and college rodeo. Some of them go on to

Saddle-bronc riding, National Finals Rodeo, Las Vegas, Nevada

compete professionally, either full-time or on weekends. Others become rodeo announcers, rodeo secretaries, event timers, judges, or stock contractors. And still others, as the song suggests, really do go on to become "doctors and lawyers and such," rather than cowboys and cowgirls. At any rate, rodeo as a youth activity will always beat hanging out at the local convenience store on Saturday nights.

In the past, most rodeo contestants came from ranch-related backgrounds, but cowboys today are just as likely to have been raised in the city. In a largely urban culture filled with avenues for getting into trouble, youth rodeo is one way parents can keep the kids busy and let them feel the exhilaration of competition and accomplishment. The family that ropes together, stays together, or so they say. For many, the "ranch" may be only an acre in suburbia, but at the rodeo they're part of the legend and lore of the West. They're back on the land with horses and cattle.

"We just want to give our kids something to remember, after they've grown up," said Professional Rodeo Cowboys Association (PRCA) bull rider Jim Watkins, as he saddled horses for his children one year at the American Junior Rodeo Association Finals in Snyder, Texas. For years, Jim and his family have traveled throughout Texas on weekends, hauling to youth rodeos.

Another rodeo parent, Butch Morgan—a part-time PRCA roper and former trick rider, with one daughter out of the nest and married, a teenage son who ropes, and a younger daughter involved with Quarter Horse shows—thought back over the last ten years. "If I would have saved all the money spent on horses, trucks, trailers, gear, plus gasoline and entry fees, I could be playing golf at the country club

today, and I'd have a Mercedes in the garage and a boat on the lake," he said. "The house would be paid for, and I could probably retire. But ... who wants all that?"

Rodeo is an expensive sport on all levels of competition. At each contest there emerges a relatively small number of winners compared with the majority of those who didn't win. But there is always another rodeo, another day to compete and perhaps win. The cowboys talk about the importance of maintaining a good attitude, keeping spirits up during a string of cold runs, hoping the check doesn't bounce until they can make it to the next rodeo or the one after that. The victory, when it comes, is sweet. Riding a tough bronc or bull for a high score and first place, tying a calf in eight seconds flat, making a three-second run in steer wrestling ... winning is great!

The prize money is nice, too. It helps pay the bills and enables a cowboy or cowgirl to continue rodeoing. "Rodeo gets in your blood," is an old expression, often used to explain why it's more important to get back on the road than to work around the house. The pros drive and fly to a hundred or more rodeos a year.

Rodeo is like golf, in a way. There are the top professionals who make a living at it, and there are many more who devote a lot of time to the game as a hobby. Team roping, in particular, is the most popular event with part-timers. On any night of the week in summer, team-roping jackpots are held throughout North America.

The event involves a header and heeler, both horseback. The header ropes the Mexican Corriente steer around the horns and leads him across the arena while the heeler moves in to rope the steer's hind legs. Time is stopped when the steer is caught at both ends with ropes taut, horses facing one

Steer
wrestling at the National Finals
Rodeo, Las Vegas, Nevada

Tom
Moorhouse and partner team roping
at the Texas Ranch Roundup, spring
gathering, Vernon, Texas

another. Fastest time wins. Team roping, more than any other event, relates to actual ranch work. Heading and heeling a cow in the open, for example, is one way to immobilize her for veterinary treatment.

Roping is fun, and roping clubs abound. State and regional rodeo associations also hold their own contests and keep track of the individual event standings for year-end awards—usually buckles. There are rodeo associations for law officers, and there are prison rodeos for inmates; there's a national military rodeo association for servicemen and their families. The most prominent youth associations include National Little Britches Rodeo Association and American Junior Rodeo Association. There's also the National High School Rodeo Association and National Intercollegiate Rodeo Associ-

ation. The PRCA, with headquarters in Colorado Springs, is the oldest and largest rodeo organization, and it sponsors the most lucrative of the pro circuits, with some 600 rodeos sanctioned annually and $16 million in prize money. Nearly $2 million of that is at stake in the PRCA's National Finals Rodeo alone. Another pro circuit, not as old or as large as the PRCA, is the Professional International Rodeo Association, based in Pauls Valley, Oklahoma. The Canadian Professional Rodeo Association, in Calgary, works closely with the PRCA.

Organized rodeo began with a forerunner of the PRCA, which for years was named simply the Rodeo Cowboys Association. Before that, when it was formed in 1936, it was the Cowboys' Turtle Association. ("We were slow as turtles gettin' organized," is one version of the reasoning behind the name.) The cowboys that year banded together and went on strike for more prize money at the Boston Garden Rodeo, in Massachusetts. So, the western sport was actually first organized by the cowboys while they were in the East. Dues were collected, files kept in a car trunk, and slowly the rules of rodeo were standardized.

Standard events today include bareback riding, saddle-bronc riding, bull riding, calf roping, and steer wrestling. In some states, at PRCA rodeos, team roping is also a standard—or required—event. Rough-stock events (the two bucking-horse contests and bull riding) involve eight-second rides that are evaluated by two rodeo judges who each mark the animal from 1 to 25 points, according to how well he bucked, and the rider from 1 to 25 on how well he rode. The points are combined, for a total possible score of 100, but the highest scores to date in the PRCA include the 93 in bareback that Joe Alexander scored on Marlboro at Cheyenne in 1974, the 95 in saddle bronc that Doug Vold scored on Transport at Meadow Lake, Saskatchewan, in 1979, and the 98 in bull riding scored by Denny Flynn on Red Lightning at Palestine, Illinois, in 1979.

Calf roping and steer wrestling (or "bulldoggin' ") are strictly timed events. Steer roping, in which a Corriente is roped around the horns then tripped to the ground and hog-tied, is one of the original events, as is

Bareback riding, Cheyenne Frontier Days Rodeo, Wyoming

Steer wrestling, Cheyenne Frontier Days Rodeo, Wyoming

saddle-bronc riding, but the sport is seen only in a couple dozen PRCA rodeos.

Women's barrel racing is one of the most popular events with spectators. Race a horse around three barrels in a cloverleaf pattern and cross the finish line. Fastest time wins. The women have their own Women's Professional Rodeo Association, headquartered at Spencer, Oklahoma, and in addition to sanctioning barrel racing at PRCA rodeos, they also sanction a relatively

small number of "all-girl" rodeos, with events that include two-handed riding in bareback and bull riding.

Some rodeos have specialty events, like wild-cow riding, calf riding (for children), and wild-horse racing. Chuck-wagon racing is a hairy event, especially popular in Canada.

There is an abundance of rodeo schools these days, and they're held throughout the country, particularly in spring. Top profes-

sionals have become teachers, who schedule three- or five-day schools, for a fee, complete with practice livestock. Anyone who wants to rodeo can begin by learning the basics of safety and success. Learning to win consistently is a different matter, something that comes with experience. The top winners in rodeo invariably possess a strong desire to win, a tolerance for pain, and a willingness to set aside creature comforts in order to "stay on the road." Retired bull

rider Jerome Robinson says that in order for a cowboy to qualify for the National Finals, to be among the top fifteen winners in his particular event, rodeo must be the most important thing in his life. Jerome qualified in bull riding eleven times between 1970 and 1981.

Jim Shoulders's famous quote, "I'd rather have a little luck than all the ability in the world," alluded to the gambling side of rodeo. Jim rodeoed from the late 1940s into

Cowboys
taping up, Salinas Rodeo, California

some insights on the subject. He was raised on a high-desert ranch near Winnemucca, Nevada, participated in rodeo as a calf roper, worked for stock contractor Bob Cook, and became a rodeo announcer. He has worked behind the scenes with rodeo committees and the PRCA board of directors; he knows the cowboys and what motivates them. Today, at age forty, Bob Tallman is the best-known voice of rodeo.

Bob has a syndicated radio program, "The Great American Cowboy," heard on hundreds of stations around the country. He has also provided commentary for many of the National Finals telecasts. And he is host of another show, rapidly gaining popularity, "The American Farmer," heard throughout much of America.

Bob has also come full circle. He started out on the ranch, went to the bright lights of big-time rodeo and broadcasting, and several years ago returned to the land. He, wife Kristin, and teenage daughter Nicole live on their combination farm and ranch in Oregon. The place consists of more than 800 acres, a portion of which is leased. It's a diverse operation, and it's turning a profit. Bob continues to announce rodeos, he has a broadcasting studio in his home and another in Eugene, and he runs the farm and ranch with no small measure of help from Kristin, two hired men, and a computer. Rodeo, broadcasting, and agriculture are intertwined for Bob, and they actually help one another.

Looking back on his life, Bob recalls his first ten years on the Nevada ranch: "I don't remember a lot about that time, except that times were tough, nothing came easy, and my dad did everything the hard way. But he did it with his hands. Then we moved to town, and that's when rodeo took over for me."

the mid '60s, and amassed a record sixteen world championships. His winnings kept a ranch together in Oklahoma and raised a family. Of course, he had the ability to take advantage of whatever luck came his way, but his point is well taken—rodeo *is* always a gamble. A man pays his own way down the road, puts up his entry fee, and takes whatever stock is drawn for him. More than money is at stake; rodeo is a dangerous game, a rough contact sport. Arena deaths are rare, but injuries are common—broken arms and legs, sometimes broken necks. The PRCA has a contestant insurance program, and for years the Justin Boot Company has underwritten a sports-medicine team that attends many of the major rodeos.

So why does anyone, whether he comes from a ranch or from town, want to be a rodeo cowboy?

Bob Tallman of Baker, Oregon, has

Calf roping,
Reno Rodeo, Nevada

Bob wanted to compete in a sport. He tried football, basketball, baseball. "They didn't work," he says. "It was all team. If I did poorly and the team won, I still got a share of the credit, which was hard to understand. If I did well but the team lost, I shared in defeat. I had a chance to excel in track, and that worked pretty good, because it was one on one. But along came rodeo, and I knew I wanted to be a cowboy."

Bob says that Larry Mahan, six-time world champion all-around cowboy, was a great influence on his life. "Until I met Larry Mahan, I really didn't know what my worth was to the rodeo industry, or how much the rodeo business could mean to me," he says. "The first guy who really took hold of me was Bob Cook, and then came Mahan. He proved to me that being a champion was not simply winning first all the time. He convinced me that if I considered myself a champion each day—at whatever I did— then I would become a champion. If I announced rodeos in a professional, championship style, with 'gold-buckle' goals, then I was a champion in my own part of the rodeo business. Mahan changed my life, and I credit him with a lot of my style in doing the things I do.

"There were others who came along, of course, like Peter Powell, who put me into the business end of broadcasting. Through all those things the rodeo business was excellent, and still is today. The opportunities in rodeo are still there for people who want to take advantage of them. But there are many people who think everything is going to come to them overnight, and it doesn't happen that way. Kristin and I went through a heck of a lot of doing with a whole lot less until any of those things started to happen."

A rodeo contestant feels a surge of adrenaline before he competes, and so does the announcer—at least Bob does. He found himself getting "up" for each performance, and he would do his homework, too. Bob would tell the crowd something about each contestant, the individual bucking styles and records of the broncs and bulls; he encouraged the crowds to cheer the cowboys on, to applaud their triumphs, to sympathize with those who met with defeat in the arena. He helped the spectators enjoy the rodeo to the fullest, and he helped to keep the show moving.

The crowds responded to his enthusiasm, and the rodeo contracts poured in. In 1982 he announced 312 performances, more than he has ever announced before or since. Ironically, Bob feels he was "the only one who didn't get something good out of that year. I made a little more money and practically killed myself doing it. I had gone so hard, so fast, that I didn't realize what was happening to me. I went through a couple periods of burnout before I even knew what burnout was."

In 1983, Bob found himself waking up at 2:30 or 3 A.M., unable to sleep. He would get out of bed and sit down with a legal tablet and box of pencils, jotting down notes, cutting up squares of paper, building imaginary pastures and fields and fencelines . . . farming and ranching.

"I decided it was time to take what I was given, a gift from my parents, who are agricultural types, and put that back into my heart, and see if my heart and mind would make it all work."

The Tallmans moved to a house on forty acres; the forty acres turned into eighty, then one-sixty, and continued to grow. "As soon as we were starting to get settled, the broadcasting and commercial business took off. For a while, I wondered

Bull riding,
Elko Rodeo, Nevada

Bob
Tallman at his Bandana Ranch in
Baker, Oregon

if I'd made the right move." He quit worrying about whether he should be in New York or Los Angeles once he built a broadcasting studio at home. He cut back on his rodeo announcing and started to enjoy that part of his life again; and the radio programs flourished, though there are always ups and downs that seem to go with the industry.

"Bob Eubanks [the TV game-show host and part-time team roper] told me one time that the radio and TV business is a lot like life—it's fatal. You're hot one day, cold the next, and I saw that was true. Well, the only thing I find constant is Mother Nature. I can count on her. I know that when it's cold and frozen on the mountain, the creek

doesn't run too high, and when it's hot and the snow is melting, we've got plenty of water. The grass will grow here under all circumstances, the bulls will breed the cows, the cows are going to have calves, and when everything else is going bad, I can go out in a field and do something, and get a feeling of accomplishment."

On his "American Farmer" radio program, Bob talks about optimism in agriculture. He conducts interviews with farmers and ranchers throughout the country, "everyone from catfish farmers in Alabama to pickle growers in Lodi, California. I'm learning about agriculture on the telephone, through interviews, and talking to America about it—and turning right around and using the same products and techniques on my own land. I've been fortunate enough to tie in my farming and ranching with what I do as a broadcaster. And the rodeo business is what started it all, and what helps sustain it all."

Bob admits that if he "had to wait for a fall market for calves or a spring market to sell pairs, we couldn't do it. You can't go buy a ranch today and start it on ranch income alone. No way. And if I didn't have Kristin and some good friends with computers, and a good herdsman like Jeff Nauman, and a good hired man in Dennis Chapman, who can fix anything and everything, I still couldn't do it. The rodeo announcing and broadcasting businesses help sustain the ranch, and being on the ranch rejuvenates me." Bob intends for his purebred Braford operation, his Quarter Horse operation, his diversified farming operation, to get better and better. "The day will come when I'll be partly in rodeo—and still love it—quite a bit in radio and commercial work, and wholly into agriculture.

Bob Tallman wasn't the only person influenced by Larry Mahan. In the years Larry reigned as King of the Cowboys—

Team roping, Peppertree Ranch, Santa Ynez, California

1966 through 1970, and again as all-around champ of the world in 1973—he influenced a whole generation of rodeo cowboys and spectators. He had charisma. He had the ability to ride barebacks, saddle broncs, and bulls equally well.

His career began at home in Brooks, Oregon. Larry, as a youngster, got the idea to use a stool to climb on top the family's milk cow; a friend opened the barn door, and the cow bolted outside with Larry astride. When he was twelve years old, Larry won six dollars and a belt buckle in a kids' calf-riding contest. Rodeo and Larry Mahan would never be the same.

"I knew early on that I really wanted to do something in rodeo, that I wanted to be successful," he says. "And I went through some lean years, too, in the beginning."

He joined the Rodeo Cowboys Association at age nineteen and won $5,641 for the entire year, working the three rough-stock events. For a while, he hauled his own practice bronc. Larry would arrive at

a rodeo well before the scheduled performance, unload the half-broke horse from his trailer, and make a practice ride inside the arena. The horse would buck just enough to help Larry practice his spurring lick. He had a very real desire to win, partly because he had a wife and young family to support.

Larry won just over $12,000 in rodeo the following year. In 1965 he was crowned world champion bull rider; he also finished seventh for the all-around with total earnings of $24,000. The other cowboys called him "Bull."

His first all-around championship came in 1966, and that was the year he also became the first man to qualify for the National Finals Rodeo in all three rough-stock events, a feat he repeated for the next four years. He set the pace in rodeo, and it was fast. He piloted his own airplane back and forth across the country, and rode and won in places like San Francisco, Denver, Cheyenne, Calgary, Houston, New York City . . . and in places like Walden, Colorado—big rodeos and small. Larry was the first cowboy to win more than $50,000 in a single season—1967. He conquered a speckled bull named Hamp at the National Finals that year and went over the mark; he predicted rodeo would continue to grow and prosper, and foresaw the day when the champions would be winning twice that amount in a year.

There were ups and a few downs. A bull stepped on his jaw and gave him a slightly crooked smile. One year the newspapers ran an AP wire photo of Larry with his foot propped up in a cast. A spur was molded into the cast, enabling him to continue riding while the fracture healed. Later in his career, he severely injured his riding arm when he hung up in the rope during bull riding at Cheyenne; he flew his plane that afternoon, with one hand, to check in with a Dallas doctor.

Shortly before that mishap, Larry had philosophized over all that was good about rodeo. "A guy feels close to nature, in a way," he said. "You spend a lot of time outside. You're competing with an animal, but you're also coping with the elements. During any week in summer, a cowboy finds himself riding under a hot afternoon sun one day, and riding in a chilly rain the next. The atmosphere around an arena is filled with smells of hay and livestock, and at the little country rodeos you get that fresh air blowing in off the fields, especially in the evening. I've seen a lot of great sunrises and sunsets, driving down the road. It's a fine life, and the people you meet and places you see make for an education you can't buy in any college."

After an unprecedented five all-around titles, plus another bull-riding championship, Larry sat out of the 1971 National Finals with another broken leg. He showed up to watch part of the rodeo, arriving at the headquarters hotel wearing hair that was moderately long, the style of those days but different from the close-cropped hair most of the other cowboys wore then. He was modeling clothes for the Jantzen line of sportswear at the time, and somehow didn't look like the majority of other cowboys. He even supported his injured leg with a wild, psychedelic-colored cane.

Larry had his detractors, people who grumbled openly that he didn't fit the cowboy mold. Larry would smile; he was still leading the way. The complaints, he realized, were most likely rooted in jealousy, rather than in genuine concern over whatever image the sport should project to the public. It seems almost trivial now, but those were the days when some rodeo hands thought it was great fun to wrestle down a hippie and take sheep shears to his long hair. Rodeo was lauded as the all-American sport, and Larry says he "didn't think it seemed very American" to abuse someone because of his appearance.

In the next few years, more and more rodeo contestants opted to wear longer hair, rather than the cropped styles of the earlier 1960s.

A young man named Phil Lyne won the all-around title the next two years, and everyone said Larry Mahan was past his prime. But in 1973 Larry made one more all-out campaign to win the big buckle, and he did it, finishing the year with $64,447 in winnings, becoming the first man to win the all-around six times. He arrived in Oklahoma City that year, where the Finals were held, driving a long, black 1960 Cadillac limousine. The amusing vehicle sported a loud orange, yellow, and purple interior, and Larry wore a chauffeur's cap while driving around town.

Jim Shoulders made the buckle presentation to Larry that year, at the conclusion of the Finals. Shoulders was a long-time rodeo stock contractor by then, and he observed that, "If this young man hadn't come along when he did, rodeo would be in deep trouble." Shoulders meant that Larry Mahan had promoted rodeo by becoming a highly visible sports figure. He had the ability to ride, and to get to more rodeos than anyone had dreamed possible, and he readily granted interviews with the press. Rodeo, by then, was attracting national sponsors who pumped dollars into the game in return for product exposure. "Rodeo gave me everything I have," Larry said. He could have said, just as honestly, that he gave rodeo everything he had.

"A guy rodeos hard like that when he wants to be champion," says Larry. "There's a certain amount of ego involved. When a cowboy is rodeoing so hard he doesn't have time to think about doing anything else, he's got to rely on an inner strength. There's a challenge there that's hard to resist. It's like getting to an extra rodeo that a lot of the others can't make that week. It's like getting on a bull everyone says is unridable, and you say to yourself, 'Watch me!'

"You're living on adrenaline, and you can get hooked on the feeling. You forget about all the long nights and miles, the bad hamburgers, living in a hotel room with six guys and two beds to shave expenses. Rodeo's a big mental game as much as a physical sport, and you build on your past successes. You don't remember the times you bucked off or got hurt, you think about the good rides, the winning."

Larry Mahan has been out of rodeo competition for a good many years, although he still team ropes for fun. He also created the successful line of Larry Mahan boots and Western clothing. His first marriage ended in divorce, and his children from that marriage—daughter, Lisa, and son, Ty—are grown. Larry is proud of them both.

Larry remarried, and he, wife Robin, and their two-year-old daughter, Eliza, own a mountain ranch in Colorado, but live on a horse ranch in Bandera County, Texas, in "the hill country" near a junction named Camp Verde. Like Bob Tallman, Larry feels close to the land. He and Robin raise cutting horses, and Larry is making headway, learning to train cutters; he's beginning to place in the major cutting contests.

He remembers his first win on a horse Rex Cauble had given him. Cauble, owner of the famous world-champion cutting horse, Cutter Bill, had given Larry a horse named Doc's Dexter, and the win came at a small cutting contest at the Cutter Bill Arena, in the spring of 1985.

"It was 3 A.M., and there I was," recalled Larry. "I'd been out of the rodeo arena for eight years, at least off the bulls and barebacks. I was relatively successful in the Western apparel business, enough so that most people in my position wouldn't be up at that hour when it was about twenty-five degrees inside, waiting to show a cutting horse in the 500 novice class. That's for the riders who haven't won $500 yet. It was also the last class at the show, and there were three or four entered. My turn to cut finally arrived, and I felt the pressure mounting. I might have blacked out a little, because I don't remember all the details, but I know I didn't lose a cow, and won the event. Robin had already 'froze out' to the motor home, and didn't hear the announcer say I had won the contest for ninety-some dollars. I've yet to forgive her for not being there, because I felt just like

I'd become the National Finals Rodeo bull riding champ.

"It's a great feeling to find another sport that lets me put on my chaps again and, hopefully, keep them on for many years to come."

Larry once said, when he was just starting in the cutting-horse business, that he wouldn't be consumed by cutting like he was by rodeo. After that first win, his outlook changed. The spark to succeed had rekindled.

"I don't feel I will hit the road as I did in rodeo, but the desire to compete and win has been taken off the shelf and dusted off. I've found that cutting, just like rodeo, requires total dedication and determination to become a consistent winner. Fortunately, I don't have to live cutting every waking hour, as I did rodeo. I'm able to channel what I learned from rodeo into cutting during those times of the day I'm working at cutting. That alone gives me time to take care of other parts of my life, which are also important.

"Looking back, I miss the way I had to push myself to reach the goals I had set in rodeo. When I'd hit a cold streak, and had already entered five rodeos for the rest of the week, I'd often want to 'chuck it to 'em'—just go home. But that inner force would push me on. I'd figure I had ridden into the slump, and the best way to get out of it was to ride out.

"I miss the freedom I found in Old Goldie, flying across the Rockies from a small rodeo in Oregon to the Calgary Stampede, competing there in the afternoon, then back to, perhaps, Spokane, Washington, or Butte, Montana, that same evening. The experiences of winning and losing, learning from both . . . I realize that I received a great deal more from rodeo

than just buckles. Everyday success would depend on self-improvement, physically and mentally, and maintaining a perfect attitude. When you're tired from travel, you learn to 'bear down' when it's time to ride, and think of nothing but making that perfect ride. That's all behind me now, but I wouldn't trade those rodeo years for anything."

Larry Mahan training a two-year-old cutting horse at his ranch in Colorado

RELUCTANT HEROES

Stuart Anderson
Black Angus Cattle Company Ranch
Thorp, Washington

In the beginning, I loved ranching because it was the opposite of a very social, people-oriented way of life. As time passed, I loved the challenge—it's never predictable. Mostly, I love the outdoors, the fresh air, and the changing ways of nature.

John J. Ascuaga
Double J.A. Land & Livestock
Nevada and California
John Ascuaga's Nugget Hotel–Casino
Sparks, Nevada

Of the many things I have been associated with during my life, the people I have met, people I have worked with, and the challenges I have faced, nothing compares with this other world of mine—ranching. There is nothing today that gives me as much pleasure as I have received from being in the livestock industry. It means a great deal to me that we still have people whose handshake means something; with a handshake, a deal is made. The majority of the people who make their living from the earth and livestock really have a deeper appreciation of life.

John
Ascuaga, Double J. A. Land &
Livestock, California and Nevada

Fog hangs
over the ranch country of Eureka
County, California.
opposite

Malcolm Baldrige
Monte Prieto Ranch
Mountainair, New Mexico

Mac loved the physical elements of ranching: the human strength, the work with horses and cattle, the open spaces, the solitude, the freedom of movement, the absence of distractions, and the perspective provided by vast natural surroundings. And Mac admired the ranchers who meet the challenge of making a living in a rugged, physical environment. He respected the self-sufficiency, the independence coupled with an ability to rely on neighbors, the focus, and the perseverance of people who choose ranching as a way of life. He appreciated the honesty of people who look beyond rank or position, who look instead at actions and character, integrity, and simplicity. Simplicity meant a lot to Mac—in word, it showed clarity of thought; in deed, it indicated a well-defined goal. For him, the quiet open spaces of a ranch provided a beautiful backdrop for independent, fair, and honest people. Mac would probably say you couldn't ask for much more than that.

—Molly Baldrige
—Megan Baldrige Murray

Rob and Peggy Brown
R. A. Brown Ranch
Throckmorton, Texas

Ranch life is the only life we know. Our grandfathers and great-grandfathers were ranchers; I'm the daughter of a rancher, and Rob's the son of a rancher. I married a rancher, our son is a rancher and married to the daughter of a rancher, our daughter is married to a rancher, and from all indications our two younger children will always be tied to the ranching industry, too. We all love the country, the very closeness of nature, the freedom of space and openness—a rainbow, a sunrise, and a sunset are just a little closer in the countryside. The pioneer spirit runs deep in our veins, and it is a life we inherited and love and hope to perpetuate. Our cowboys are deeply rooted in pioneer traditions, and though lots of things change, our cowboys are grassroots, salt-of-the-earth folks dependent on Mother Nature and daily reminded of this fact—be it sunshine, rain, or the lack of it. We are tied to the soil and what it yields; together, we care about the land and realize there isn't any more being made. We must be practical in taking care of it and managing it for the next generations. Texas cowboys' hearts are as big as the West Texas sky, and the ones we are fortunate to work with every day are without a doubt the cream of the crop.

The Self family and the Brown family have worked side by side for three generations and over fifty years. That relationship is something unique, and we all believe it is this joint venture that makes it all work for the R. A. Brown Ranch.

Rob and
Peggy Brown, R. A. Brown Ranch,
Throckmorton, Texas

George Self
R. A. Brown Ranch
Throckmorton, Texas

Born into ranch life, I grew up with a special feeling for the country. Being able to work with horses and cattle is a challenge every day, and no two days are the same. It takes a special kind of dedication to live on a ranch. The hours are long, the work is hard, and the pay is small, but you feel good about what you accomplish. You appreciate nature a lot more and are witness to many of God's creations that not many people see.

The ability to use your skills and knowledge working with the horses you break and train, or working cattle, helping an ol' cow calve, and bring a new life into this old world, gives you a satisfaction down inside no one else can feel. To be able to live in close harmony with nature is a self-rewarding and fulfilling life. I guess I am one of the lucky ones to be a part of the Western heritage and help it live on. It don't get no better than this.

George A. Brown
Brown Ranch
Channing, Texas

I like the atmosphere of rural living; getting up during the early hours of the day to hear coyotes howling instead of brakes squealing is an advantage I have over my city brothers. Constantly striving to breed better and better horses is a goal I continually pursue. I like being a steward of the soil; keeping the grassland in as good and clean shape as the Father created it is another of my ranching responsibilities by which I am challenged. Raising my children and grandchildren to know about nature and how it should be revered is a fringe benefit I plan to leave as my personal legacy to ranching. Never do I want it to be said that I took more from the profession than I left.

George Brown, Brown Ranch, Channing, Texas

Deborah
Chastain, Cedar Creek Ranch,
Saratoga, Wyoming

Deborah B. Chastain
Cedar Creek Ranch
Saratoga, Wyoming

William Clark
Clark Company
Paso Robles, California

In 1947 I read a book entitled *The Complete Rancher* by Russell Bennett. That did it. I had to have a ranch in Wyoming. The fact that I knew nothing about the business didn't deter me. I don't regret for a moment my decision. Each day is different and *never* what you planned to do! When the sun is up, so am I. It would be awful to miss a second of what Wyoming has to show me. It's the mountains, the river, the sage brush, and mostly it's people who have taught me to appreciate my new way of living.

Not unlike that black colt down the canyon, some of us were simply lucky enough to be born and bred in the same kind of canyon. In other words, we didn't choose it, we were fortunate enough to have been chosen for it. We choose to continue a tradition typifying the best of America. Put differently by my grandfather, "We moved in and never made enough to move out."

Charlie Daniels
Twin Pines Ranch
Mt. Juliet, Tennessee

ALL THINGS CONSIDERED

All things considered, I guess you could say that ranching these days makes about as much sense as picking a fight with a rutting grizzly bear or betting your hard-earned money that a politician's gonna tell the truth, the whole truth, and nothing but the truth.

Ranchers fight weather, beef prices, and ridiculous import quotas on a daily basis, not to mention predators and dry water holes.

They get up before the sun does and spend their days in heat, cold, snow, wind, and downright aggravation.

They spend their nights poring over accounts that reflect an ever-dwindling profit margin and hoping that they can coax just one more year out of that old pick-up truck.

It's genteel insanity and a gamble at best. So why would a man spend his life in the middle of nowhere with the odds so heavily against him?

Don't ask that question unless you've heard the whistle of houlihans in the pre-dawn stillness or topped a hill at first light and seen the dew diamonds sparkling in a thousand-acre pasture.

Don't question it unless you've smelled the sage stomped out of horses' hooves or tasted old Cookie's coffee.

Don't judge until you've scratched your chaps on catclaw or watched calves frolicking and kicking up their heels under God's blue, blue western sky.

And if you haven't seen that full silver moon shining down out of sky so clear that each star is as brilliant as a prize emerald, don't you even say a word.

How could you know, if you've never heard the squeak of saddle leather or dallied off a runaway.

Come and sit at my fire. Listen to the old men talk about the days of the big outfits, when the range was wild and un-fenced.

Come and ride my gentlest horses and watch the boys sitting tall and proud in their saddles, proud to be a cowboy.

Come and sleep under my stars, drink from my mountain streams. Come and touch my world.

And then, maybe, just maybe, you'll understand why there's no other way of life for us, win, lose, or draw.

Dear Lord, may there always be an open range, some cows, and a good solid horse for me to ride. May there always be a ranch.

Charlie
Daniels, Twin Pines Ranch,
Mt. Juliet, Tennessee

A. D. Davis
Big Horn Ranch
Cowdrey, Colorado

Les & Linda Davis
C S Ranch
Cimarron, New Mexico

I was introduced to ranch life as a boy eleven years old, when I had a job taking care of cattle for a rancher. I loved the outdoors and freedom of the open spaces and decided then I would one day own a ranch. The cattle business was my goal. After thirty years of ranch ownership, it is still my first love. The magnificent mountains, pure streams, rich meadows, and peaceful beauty of the Big Horn Ranch are bountiful rewards for the many years of hard work. I enjoy sharing my experiences and knowledge with other ranchers. We are kindred souls.

Les and Linda Davis family, C S Ranch, Cimarron, New Mexico

We inherited a deep love for the land. Les's grandfather, Frank Springer, established the C S Ranch near Cimarron, New Mexico, in 1873. Linda's great grandfather founded the nucleus of the Tequesquite Ranch in that valley close to Albert, New Mexico, in 1876. Today, our six children are on the C S Ranch and involved in all phases of its operation. They seem to have inherited the energy, interest, and tenacity to strive to survive in this challenging business.

Ranchers are the true environmentalists in society today. We derive our livelihood from grass marketed in the form of beef cattle. Hazards of nature, drought, dust storms, blizzards, fire, flood, disease, and infestations are all part of our daily life. Isolation and modest economic returns accompany this way of life. Cowboying is a lonely skill not learned from a book, but an art form for which the individual must have an aptitude.

We hope to convey to our sixth ranching generation, our grandchildren, the satisfaction and sense of accomplishment that accompanies success in the livestock industry. Like the preceding generations, they will need initiative and determination, but will always have the realization that they are involved in the production of wholesome food for an ever-expanding population. Their ranching friends and neighbors, they will find, as we have, are a wonderful and special breed of people—hard-working, independent, and patriotic, with close family ties.

Wright Dickinson Family
Lazy V D Land & Livestock Co.
Browns Park, Colorado

A. W. Dickinson III (father): I was born into this way of life. I like it, and I'm fortunate to be able to do what I like to do the best, and that is to be a rancher.

Polly Dickinson (mother): I didn't choose the life, I chose the man—and am thankful for them both.

T. Wright Dickinson (eldest son): When God made this world, He didn't finish it. He left that to us, to make it a better place than we found it. Since 1885, when my great-grandfather came here, my family has tried to make this a better, more productive place. I feel fortunate to be the fourth generation entrusted with the care of this land and its animals. I feel great responsibility to those that came before me to continue their work. I enjoy doing what I do, working with my family. Hopefully, I will leave this place better than I found it and to another generation.

Jean Dickinson (eldest daughter): I love being part of something this good that has lasted so long. This life is really living; that is why it is so good. I get to breathe fresh air every day, and I'm very thankful.

DeeDee Dickinson (daughter): I like that I've helped preserve and maintain a part of agriculture's history. Because of the past and present, I am able to look to the future with an open mind and enthusiasm.

Marc Dickinson (son): I love it. I love being isolated. The ranch is my life. I've heard people say they love the big city; well, I love the ranch. The less people that are around me, the better. There's a town ninety miles away; that's fine with me!

The family: Making a living from the land and cattle is an honest and wonderful way to raise a family and be a family.

Roy F. Fulton
IAQUA Ranch
Eureka, California

I was lucky enough to be born into a ranching family. I guess I was born with a love for the land and livestock. It's hard work, and I like the honest, hard-working people you meet in this way of life. I like what I'm doing. It has treated me well, and that's why I have stayed in the ranching business.

Roy and Betty Fulton, Iaqua Ranch, Eureka, California

James
William and Peter Guercio, Caribou
Ranch, Nederland, Colorado

Charles C. Gates
Big Creek Ranch
Encampment, Wyoming
The Gates Corporation
Denver, Colorado

A horse to swing astride of, a trout stream to cast a fly upon, and a wide-open range tented by deep blue sky and warmed by mucho sun rays—these are the pleasures of a ranching way of life.

It has been said that nothing does more for the inside of a man than the outside of a horse, that days on a fishing stream are not subtracted from one's life calendar, and that the great out-of-doors is where one realizes humility, finds serenity, and captures fresh inspiration all at once.

It is thus a privilege to live in the West and to have the opportunity to periodically step from being a desk-chair jockey into the stirrup on a cow pony.

James William Guercio
Caribou Ranch
Nederland, Colorado

I've chosen this way of life for my children and their children. The independence of the decision-making process, the ability to implement those decisions directly with your labor in the field, and the continuing responsibilities of those decisions upon the ever-changing landscape of the marketplace offer the satisfaction and challenge I've found in no other business endeavor I've ever been involved in. There's no adjusting of the balance sheet to rendering one's achievements. It works or it doesn't. The American traditions of self-reliance, independence, and freedom are daily realizations. We've never received any government subsidy or assistance of any kind whatsoever. Any mistakes that we have made—and there's been more than a few—we've paid for with hard work, sweat, and, occasionally, tears.

God, *family*, and *country* are the defined principles of ranching, as we have come to know and live it year in and year out. I cannot think of a better order of priorities in this life to leave to our children. May God continue to bless this land and its people for as long as the grass grows and the rivers flow.

That's about it.

Ceborn (Cebe) Hanson
Big Horn Ranch
Cowdrey, Colorado

I choose to be a rancher because I like it. I like the challenge—raising hay and growing grass, producing good calves, fighting Mother Nature a lot of the time. I like the rewards, too. Spring here in the high country makes it all worthwhile, when the calves start coming and the hay and the grass start growing. I also like it when the markets are good. In ranching the responsibilities are great, but the sense of having freedom is greater.

Cebe Hanson,
Big Horn Ranch, Cowdrey, Colorado

Jim Humphreys
Pitchfork Land & Cattle Co.
Texas, Wyoming, and Kansas

I wanted to be in the producer end of the cattle industry, where you can be near to nature and enjoy God's creation and creatures, the good things of life, a family life at its best. My wife, Berneice, and I raised four children on the ranch, and they all appreciate the great opportunity they had growing up in a rural area. Ranching has given our family a wonderful opportunity to become acquainted with some mighty good folks, genuine people you can believe in and trust.

Ben Johnson
Mesa, Arizona

We have lost three things today . . . honesty, realism, and respect. I have been on my own since I was eleven years old. I was taught to live by the Golden Rule, to do unto others as you would have them do unto you. Through ranching life I have found more people who live the way I like, and ranch life has been pretty good to me. I feel that a lot of what I have to give on the screen and in life has come from the way I grew up.

Stephen J. "Tio" Kleberg
King Ranch
Kingsville, Texas

Ranching allows me the ability to be an independent thinker. Ranching combines the love of nature, land, animals, and people into a way of living. To have serenity, to see the beauty and gentleness for just a moment in a day makes it all worthwhile.

Stephen
"Tio" Kleberg, King Ranch, Kingsville,
Texas

John Lacey
Lacey & Son Cattle Ranches
Paso Robles, California

Ranching is a way of life that one must experience to understand and appreciate. I ranch because the business is a constant challenge. Each day brings new facts and circumstances that must be dealt with—without the aid of a rule book or guidelines. Ranching keeps me outdoors and gives me a hand in nature, which is very rewarding to me. Above all, the people with whom I associate are basic and down-to-earth, and their word is their bond.

John Lacey,
Lacey & Son Ranch, Paso Robles,
California

Dan Lufkin,
Oxbow Ranch, Prairie City, Oregon

Mark J. Lacey
Lacey & Son Cattle Ranches
Paso Robles, California

Dan Lufkin
Oxbow Ranch
Prairie City, Oregon

I didn't choose ranching. I was born to it. A person almost has to be, because ranching isn't a job. It's a way of life. It requires more commitment than most other jobs. Most people get to leave their jobs Friday at five o'clock. Mine is all day, every day. A person really has to love what he is doing to live with that commitment, and I do. I couldn't stand to be riding a desk and chair instead of a horse. Luckily, I had a choice. How many people on Wall Street have the view from their offices that ranchers have from theirs?

The wet-nose calf almost hidden in a pasture of wild timothy, the silent passage of a great horned owl over the moon, the majestic bald eagle seen through early morning mist in spring calving, the winter-night serenade of the coyote, the early spring iris peering through snow melt . . . freedom from people and a world of things, in never-failing partnership with a good dog and a good horse . . . harmony with oneself and the basic rhythms of life and death. For all our wondrous works and soaring dreams, we depend for life itself on six inches of soil and the fact that it rains every now and then.

Tom McGuane
Raw Deal Ranch
McLeod, Montana

I like what you see when you walk out in your yard in rural Montana. I like my children in country schools. I like to fish in the summer and hunt in the fall. I like to mess around with horses, cattle, and stock dogs. I like it whenever the hoot owls elope with the chickens.

Tom McGuane, Raw Deal Ranch, during a cutting in Big Timber, Montana

Pat Mantle
Sombrero Ranch
Craig, Colorado

I grew up in the ranching business, so I came by it natural. I like the independent life, don't have to count the clock to be at work on time. A little less government control (more all the time). You have to make your own decisions. There isn't any book that fits all operations. Ranching keeps you more active. You see a lot more old ranchers than you do old bankers (I've worn out several myself).

Pat Mantle,
Sombrero Ranch, Craig, Colorado

Watt Matthews
Lambshead & Matthews Ranches
Albany, Texas

City life just doesn't fit my program.

Watt
Matthews, Lambshead &
Matthews Ranches, Albany, Texas

Tom Moorhouse
Moorhouse Ranch Co.
Benjamin, Texas

I was born and raised in the ranching business. My grandad pastured yearlings in the Indian Nation (Oklahoma) in the 1800s. I didn't choose ranch life; I inherited it. It's probably in our blood. We love the out-of-doors, nature, and livestock. We relate best to people who know cattle and have spent most of their life horseback. We admire good horses, skilled cowboys, and the smell of mesquite wood burning. We like the business—putting beef on the consumer's table. We are always glad when the market's good and we've had ample rain. Always hoping, when we haven't. I thank God regularly that He has provided me with a ranch life and a family who loves it, too!

Tribute to Sue Moorhouse

She was my wife and best friend, and I loved her. She was a lady and a cowgirl. She could teach a Sunday school class or doctor a sick yearling. She was a ranch girl. She realized that the Lord furnishes the rain, and we furnish the labor and management. She loved the ranch, ranch people, and Mother Nature. She loved her kids and family. I've heard it said, "There is a time to move fast and a time to move slow, and only a good cowboy knows when." She knew *when*, with a cow or with people. She died last summer here at the ranch. She is buried not far from here, on the ranch. She never gave up. Thank God for the time I was allowed to spend with her.

Robert C. Norris
T-Cross Ranches
Colorado Springs, Colorado

I choose ranch life for the following reasons: Family involvement—to be with and grow with my family while enjoying my love for the outdoors (not being chained to a desk) and working with livestock, to have the freedom of choice and independence to make my own decisions, to be involved with as many facets of the industry and community as I wish. Every day brings a new challenge.

Robert C. Norris (left), T Cross Ranches, Colorado Springs, Colorado

Tom, Sue, Jed, and Jody Moorhouse, Moorhouse Ranch, Benjamin, Texas

Nicholas
Petry, Mill Iron Ranches, Saratoga,
Wyoming

Nicholas R. Petry
Mill Iron Ranches
Saratoga, Wyoming

Ranch-style living means being with confident, talented people who appreciate each
other and their work. It means a love of
the tapestry of nature: seasons, animals,
birds, water, soil, vegetation, and weather.

Bill Pruitt
Manager, Beaver Meadows Ranch
McLeod, Montana

I'm a man of the soil—a man of the outdoors. I realized as a boy that my basic nature and foundation was "of the soil," as an individual. Livestock, especially cattle and horses, are my major. But the farming, the fencing, and all the million problems and challenges that ranch life consists of are my bread and butter. I love it. So, if I can be financially successful with my first choice, I'll be the happiest and most productive to my family, community, and our great country.

Dan H. Russell
Russell Ranches
California and Nevada

I have grown up in the ranching profession, being the third generation on both sides. I've chosen to continue ranching because of the challenge, independence, and way of life it offers. It also brings you close to nature and the land, which we try to protect. Ranching certainly has its gamble: weather, price fluctuations, sickness, and infestations. It boils down to one point: it is a very demanding profession but one I would not trade for any other.

Dan Russell, Russell Ranches and Western Rodeos, California and Nevada

Fern Sawyer
Riachuela Ranch
Nogal, New Mexico

The main reason I ranch—I do not know anything else. Born and raised on a ranch, I have never wanted to do anything else. I understand cows, riding a horse, and enjoy the full life that only a ranch affords. Not much money, but a hell of a good time and life.

Charles Schreiner IV
Y. O. Ranch
Mountain Home, Texas

I choose ranch life because I think it is the best life available for me to achieve my goals according to my priorities: God, family, ranch, and country. I believe there's no better place on earth than the Y. O. Ranch to most fully utilize my God-given abilities and talents to please God, to continue to provide a fun, happy, exciting, safe place to raise my family, to be a good husband and father, to create the "Best Business Ranch in the World," to help with local and international wildlife conservation efforts, to preserve our Western heritage, and to serve my country by helping rediscover, re-establish, and reaffirm the values that brought my great-great-grandparents to Texas in 1852. I believe I can best make my mark and go to heaven by living this life, which I know best.

Fern Sawyer, Riachuela Ranch, Nogal, New Mexico

J. R. Simplot
J. R. Simplot Company
Boise, Idaho

Nobody is going to get rich in ranching today, unless they get lucky and "hit a lick" one year, then get out the next. The real profit in ranching is the romance of it all— in owning a piece of this great America. There is satisfaction in knowing you have something that contributes in growth and stabilizes in recession. It's a part of America that has served not only as a home to families, but a guardian of their roots through each generation. And it remains fertile enough to germinate the new and willing. That, I believe, is truly the essence of ranching life.

Dean Smith
Bar Double Diamond
Ivan, Texas

My great-grandfather, George W. Hill, settled on the Clear Fork of the Brazos in 1876 near Eliaseville, Texas. The ranch he settled on was passed on to me from my grandmother on my father's side, Ollie Hill Smith. She married a rancher from Ivan, Texas, named Pink Smith in 1900. They had two sons, who were both ranchers, my father, George Finis Smith, and King Smith. Currently, I own two ranches in Ivan called the Bar Double Diamond. I own these ranches because of the pioneer spirit my grandmother instilled in me. She taught me to love the land and to respect horses and cattle. My western heritage comes from the long line of ranchers who also believed in the tradition of the West and the Western spirit.

J. R. Simplot
at home in Boise, Idaho

Chuck
Sylvester, Circle Bar Ranch,
Alcova, Wyoming

Jack Sparrowk
Sparrowk Livestock
Clements, California

Charles and Kay Sylvester
Circle Bar Ranch
Alcova, Wyoming

All my life all I ever wanted to be was a cowboy. After I got to be a cowboy I decided I wanted to make some money, so I went into the cattle business. It's a tough business, but I don't want to do anything else. I like it, and I like the people in it.

Life is made more wonderful when you can combine important aspects that you personally enjoy—the great outdoors and cattle and horses. Add a little imagination, and you can relive the frontier way of life that makes up our Western heritage. Add to that the challenge of modern ranching, which is to operate a successful business and produce a quality product of modern-day beef for the consumer by overcoming the adversities of winter storms, summer droughts, and cyclical economics. Altogether, these things make ranch work exciting and rewarding.

Gordon K. Van Vleck
Plymouth, California

I was raised on the family ranch, and, as I helped with the chores, I learned that ranching can be hard work but has important rewards. I enjoyed the outdoors. I liked working with horses and cattle. I liked earning my living from the land. I came to understand the value of being your own boss. I enjoyed the company of the people I met through ranching.

Today, many friends from other professions retire to the country, buy some horses and cows, and enjoy themselves. I've had those pleasures all my life. I see no reason to change.

Dub Waldrip
Spade Ranches
Lubbock, Texas

It's sure not the money. Maybe it's the people or the way of life. I think it's the continuing anticipation—the hope or promise of things to come. We live in "next year" country.

Buster Welch
Welch Ranches
Sweetwater, Texas

Buster Welch,
Welch Ranches, Sweetwater, Texas

Ever since I was a small boy, I have loved horses, cattle, the outdoors, and doing the work that goes with them. Ranching is the most satisfying occupation in the world, when everything is going right. But it is absolutely the most demanding and brutal when things go wrong, and it will certainly discipline you. It gives you a feeling of forever; you are always looking forward to the next calf crop, the next top horse. I think it is not really a business, but an art— that has to be treated in a businesslike manner.

ACKNOWLEDGMENTS

No achievement is possible without the support, encouragement, and inspiration of family and friends. My life is abundantly blessed with exceptional people, and I am forever grateful to each of them for their continued love and friendship; here is a big hug and thank you to each of you . . .

Joe & Betty Ryan, Joannie & Jim Torrence, Brea & Robert McGrew, Cheri & Joe Bottero, Vivian McAteer, Bobbie Stone, Peter Ryan, Betsy Brawley, Helen Nelson, Don Warning, Maddie & Molly Warning, Cathy McDermott, Bobbie Mark, Jack & Janet O'Loughlin, Jim Cockman, Sandie Wernick, Jane Offers, Carol & Paul Weston, Audean & Jim Franklin, Alan & Ingaborg Hallock, Corine & Bill Back, Sarah Howard, and the Center for Attitudinal Healing.

Thank you to Chris & Fran Stritzinger, Angel & Judy Naves, Penny Bauer, Ed Rutherford, and Breazy Rosenthal for their very special support.

Thank you to Gordon Van Vleck, one of my 4-H leaders who remembered—and who helped me launch this project.

A very big thank you to all of my new friends who graciously invited me into their hearts and homes, offering me the friendship, hugs, generosity, and kindness that enabled me to complete this book . . .

Harla Dedrick, Mardie & Cebe Hanson, Radonna Long, Tad Cheyenne Schutt, Chuck & Kay Sylvester, Dan & Bobbie Russell, Lisa & Roy Shurtz, Frances & Frank Gardner, Bob, Kristen & Nicole Tallman, John Ascuaga, Ruth Jones, Paula Wright, John & Dee Lacey, Wright & Polly Dickinson Family, Buster & Sheila Welch, Bill & Lindsey Serrell, Dub Waldrip, Rob & Peggy Brown, Tom, Jody & Jed Moorhouse, Russ & Donna Burgess, Dan Lufkin, Jenny Gibbs, Brad & Pam McGarry, Tom Hovendon, Dave Shipper, Pat Mantle, John & Barb Shipley, Maggie Bentz, Roy & Betty Fulton, Helen & Stuart Anderson, Buzzy & Billie Thorpe, Jack & Catherine Algeo, Les & Linda Davis.

Thank you to all my friends at the Professional Rodeo Cowboys Association, especially Steve Fleming, Kay Blakley, T. J. Walter, Pat Florence, Patty Daly, and Commissioner Louis Cryer; also to Pat Steenberge at the National Cutting Horse Association.

Thanks to my friends at Eastman Kodak, Ken Fossan (who brilliantly handled all of my film), Hugh Richardson, and Marianne Samenko for making this project a joy to photograph.

An extra thank you to Ann Harris, Lew Keim, Steve Pickens, George Schott, and Julie Klee for their commitment and support.

Thank you to each of the wonderful and talented writers for sharing their ranching expriences through their reflective literary contributions—and for their friendship.

A special thank you to my friends at *Western Horseman* magazine, Dick Spencer, Randy Witte, and Darrell Arnold.

Thanks to each of the Reluctant Heroes for their courage, inspiration, and example, and for thoughtfully putting their feelings and observations into words.

A special thank you to all of the ranchers and their families for their warm hospitality and opportunity to visit and photograph some of the most spectacular country in the West—as well as for all of the extraordinary adventures and wonderful horses to ride . . .

CALIFORNIA
Jack Cooke & Harlan Brown, Hearst Ranch, San Simeon; Roy & Betty Fulton, Iaqua Ranch, Eureka; John & Dee Lacey, Lacey & Son Ranches, Paso Robles and Olancha; Jack & Bev Sparrowk, Sparrowk Livestock, Clements

COLORADO

Cebe & Mardie Hanson, Big Horn Ranches, Cowdrey; Jim & Lucy Guercio, Caribou Ranch, Nederland; Wright & Polly Dickinson Family, Lazy V. D. Land & Livestock Ranch, Browns Park; Jim Noffsinger, Noffsinger Ranches, Walden; Nate & Virginia Patton, Patton Ranches, Canyon City; Pat Mantle, Sombrero Ranches, Craig & Browns Park; Bob Norris, T Cross Ranches, Colorado Springs; Bill Trampe, Trampe Ranches, Gunnison

IDAHO

Jim Little, Van Deusen Ranch, Emmett; John Basabe, Simplot Land & Cattle, Grandview & Caldwell

MONTANA

Walter Haas & Bill Pruitt, Beaver Meadows Ranch, McLeod; Tom, Laurie & Annie McGuane, Raw Deal Ranch, McLeod

NEVADA

John Ascuaga & Leo Summers, Double J. A. Land & Livestock Company, Smith Valley & Jacks Valley; Roy & Lisa Shurtz, La Vaca Co. Ranch, Elko; Dan & Bobbie Russell, Russell Ranches, Eureka & Elko; Horace, Renie & Kim Smith, Cottonwood Ranch, O'Neill Basin, Wells

NEW MEXICO

Les & Linda Davis, C S Ranch, Cimarron; Fern Sawyer, Riachuela Ranch, Nogal

OREGON

Bob, Kristin & Nicole Tallman, Bandana Ranch, Baker; Dan Lufkin, Oxbow Ranch, Prairie City

TEXAS

George & Fay Brown, Brown Ranch, Channing; Rob & Peggy Brown, R. A. Brown Ranch, Throckmorton; Tio Kleberg, King Ranch, Kingsville; Watt Matthews, Lambshead & Matthews Ranches, Albany; Tom, Jody & Jed Moorhouse, Moorhouse Ranch; Roy McAdams, Twin Mountains Ranch, Baird; Buster & Sheila Welch, Welch Ranches, Sweetwater; Charles Schreiner Fam-ily, Y O Ranch, Kerrville; The National Ranching Heritage Center, Museum of Texas Tech University, Lubbock; Texas Ranch Roundup, Wichita Falls

WASHINGTON

Stuart & Helen Anderson, Black Angus Cattle Co. Ranch, Thorp; Bob Lungren, L & M Feeders, Pasco

WYOMING

Charles Gates, Charles & Shirley Dunning, Big Creek Ranch, Encampment; Deborah Chastain, Cedar Creek Ranch, Saratoga; Chuck & Kay Sylvester, Circle Bar Ranch, Alcova; Cliff Hansen, Hansen Ranch, Jackson; Nick & Nancy Petry, Mill Iron Ranches, Saratoga; Bernard & Nolene Sun, Sun Ranch, Alcova

Thank you to all of the talented folks at Abbeville Press for producing this book to the highest standards, especially Alan Axelrod, the editor, for his under-standing and guidance; Julie Rauer, the designer, for her aesthetic sense and elegant design; and to Bob Abrams for his vision.

—Kathleen Jo Ryan

INDEX